GRATEFUL DEAD AUTHENTIC GUIT

AUTHENTIC GUITAR CLASSICS VOL. 1

Artwork © Grateful Dead Productions, Inc.
Editor: Aaron Stang
Arranger: Hemme Luttjeboer

©1996 ICE NINE PUBLISHING CO., INC.
All Rights Reserved

Any duplication, adaptation or arrangement of the compositions
contained in this collection requires the written consent of the Publisher.
No part of this book may be photocopied or reproduced in any way without permission.
Unauthorized uses are an infringement of U.S. Copyright Act and are punishable by Law.

CONTENTS

BLACK PETER . . . 4

BOX OF RAIN . . . 23

CASEY JONES . . . 44

CUMBERLAND BLUES . . . 60

FRIEND OF THE DEVIL . . . 84

NEW SPEEDWAY BOOGIE . . . 106

RIPPLE . . . 124

SUGAR MAGNOLIA . . . 138

TRUCKIN' . . . 150

UNCLE JOHN'S BAND . . . 175

BLACK PETER

Words by ROBERT HUNTER
Music by JERRY GARCIA

© 1971, 1991 ICE NINE PUBLISHING CO., INC.

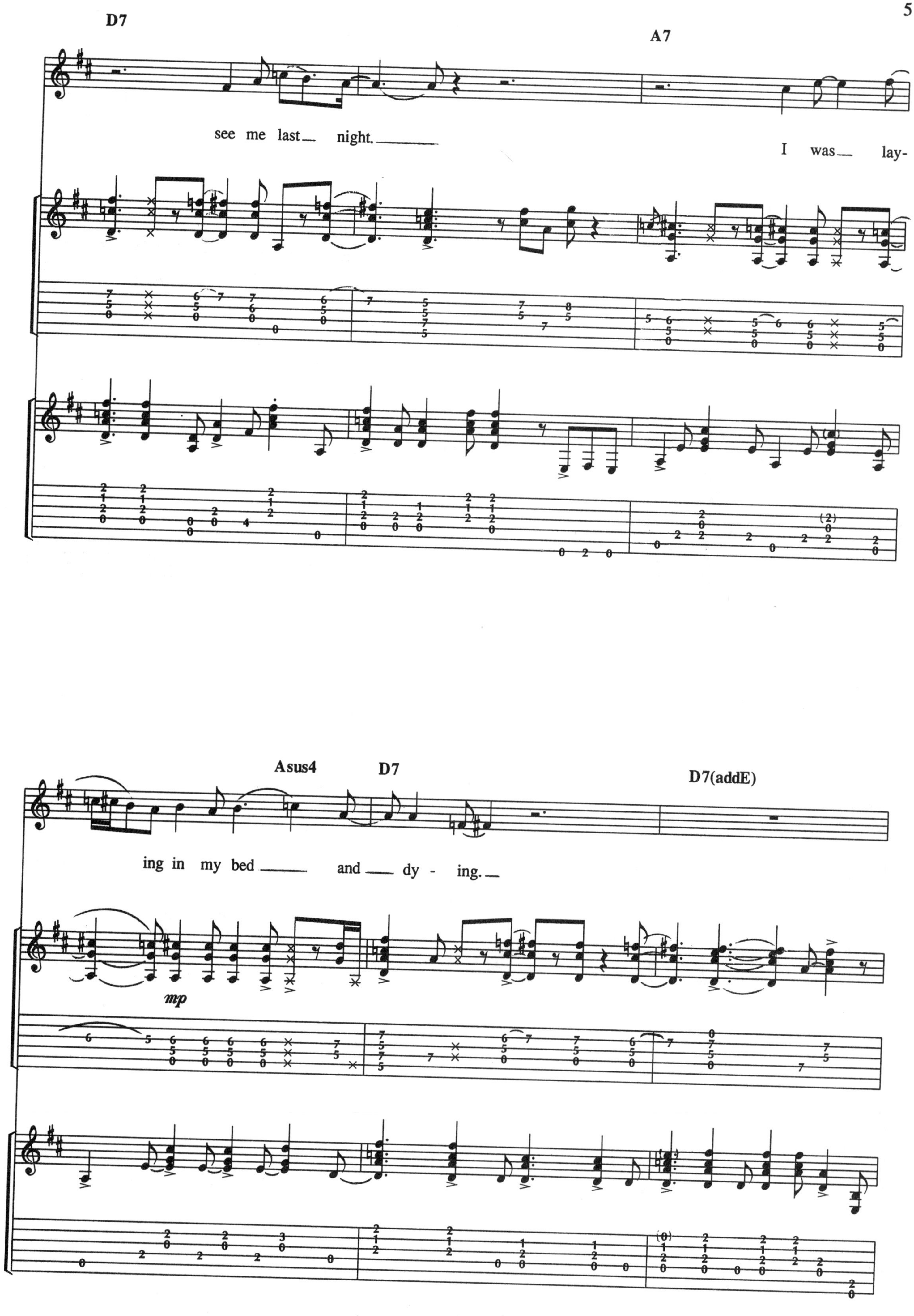
D7
A7
see me last night.
I was lay-
Asus4
D7
D7(addE)
ing in my bed and dy - ing.
mp

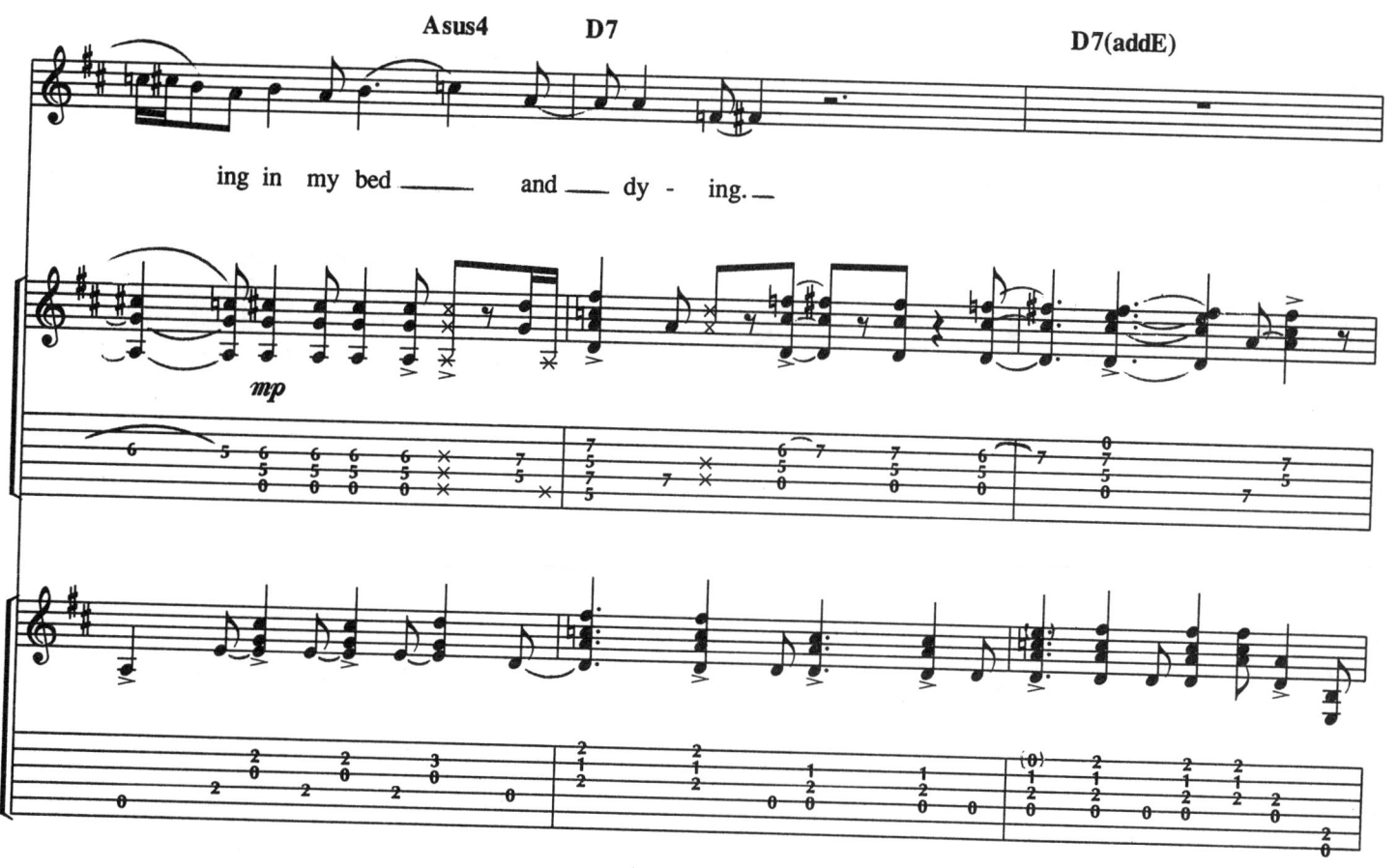

so fine.

Verse 2:

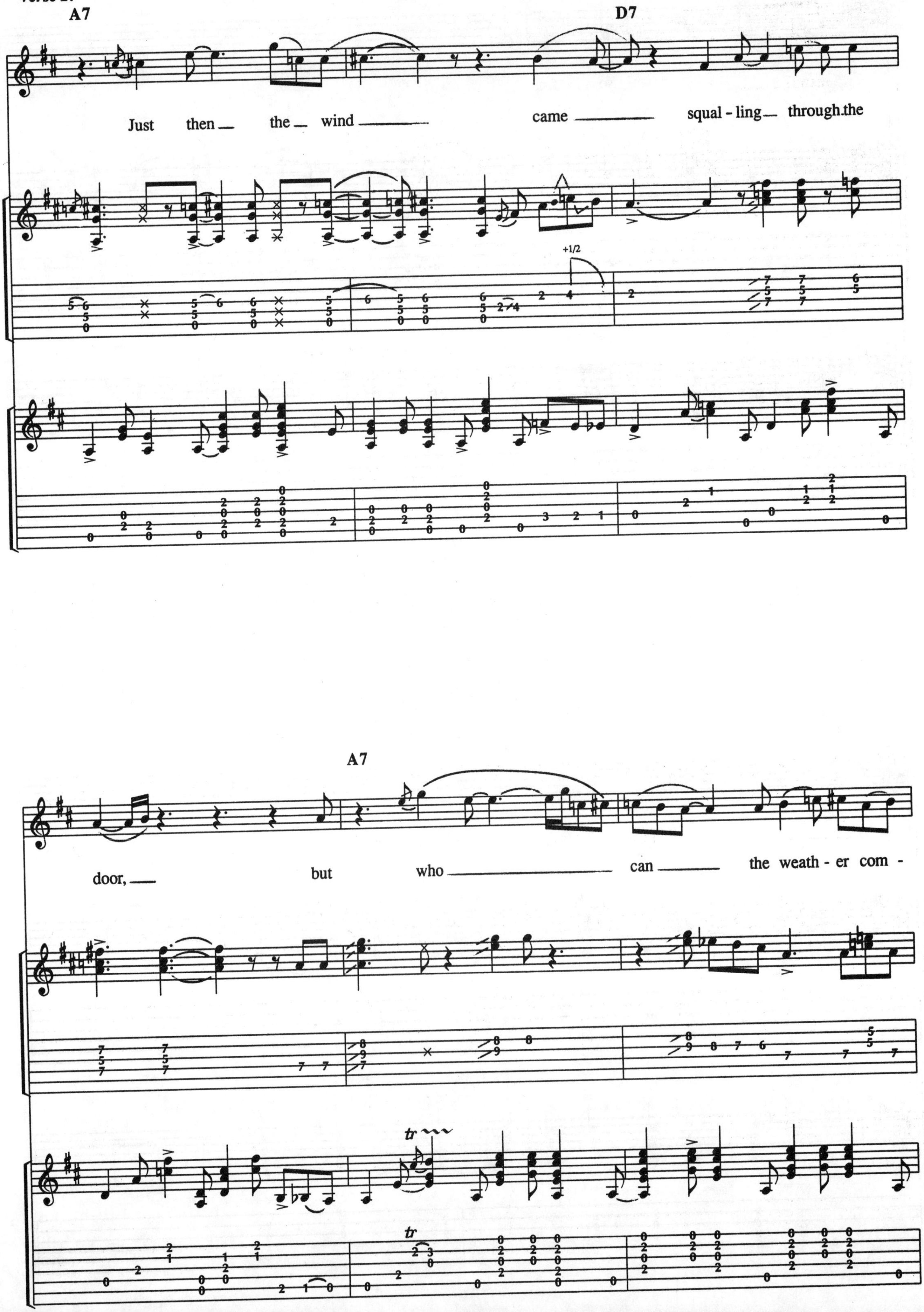
A7
D7
Just then the wind came squal - ling through.the
+1/2
A7
door, but who can the weath - er com -
tr

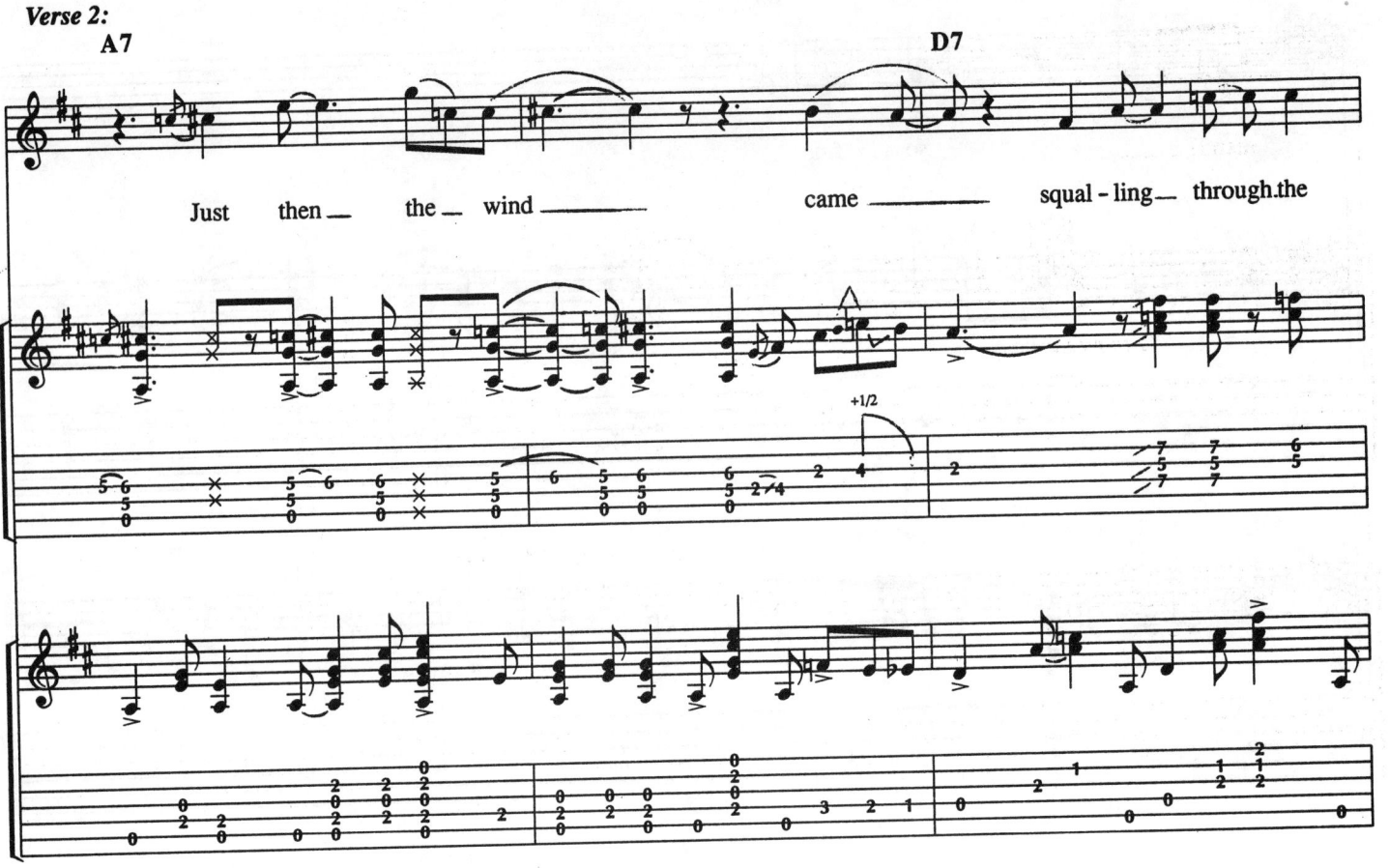

mand? Just wan-na have a lit-tle peace to die, and a

10

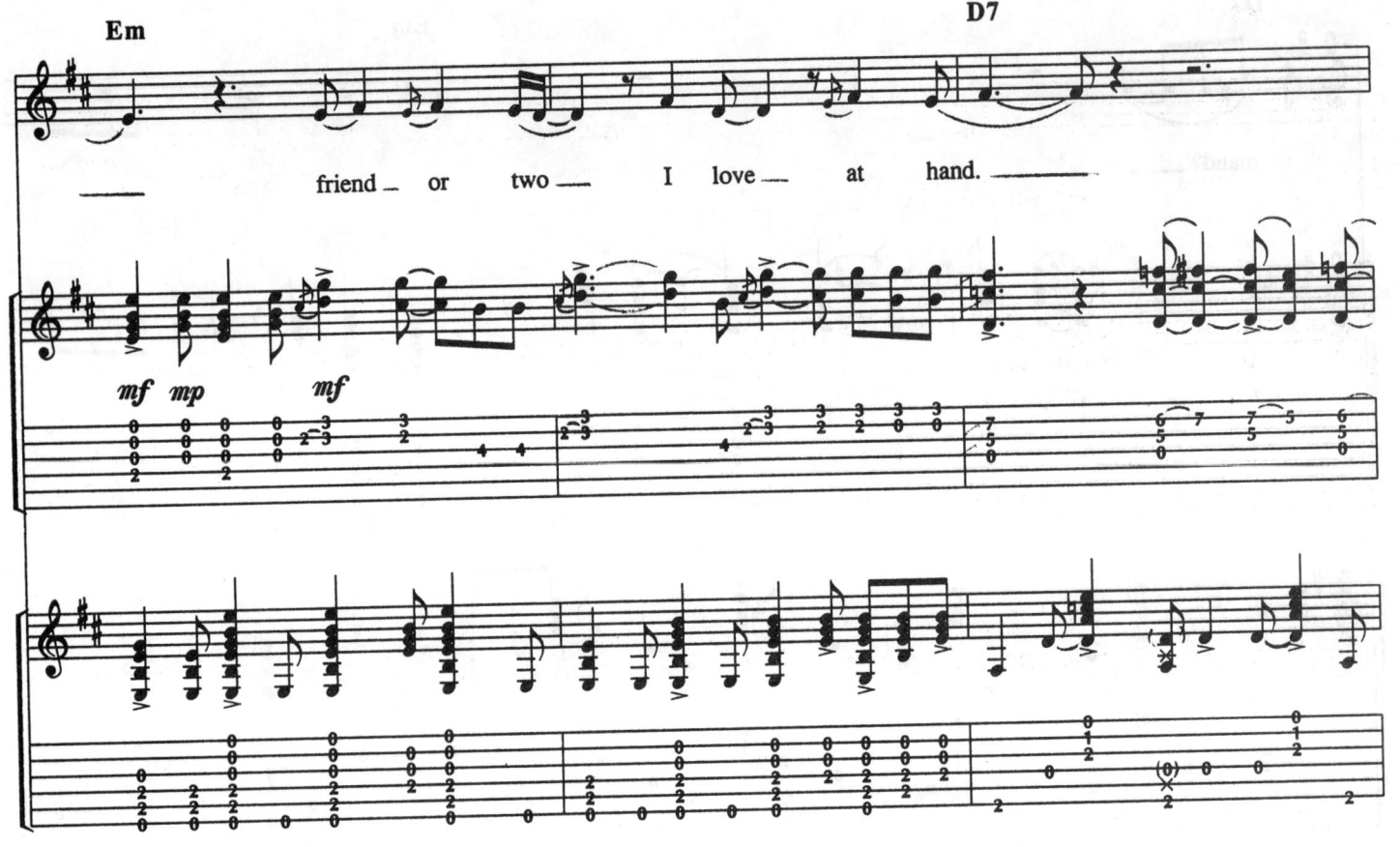

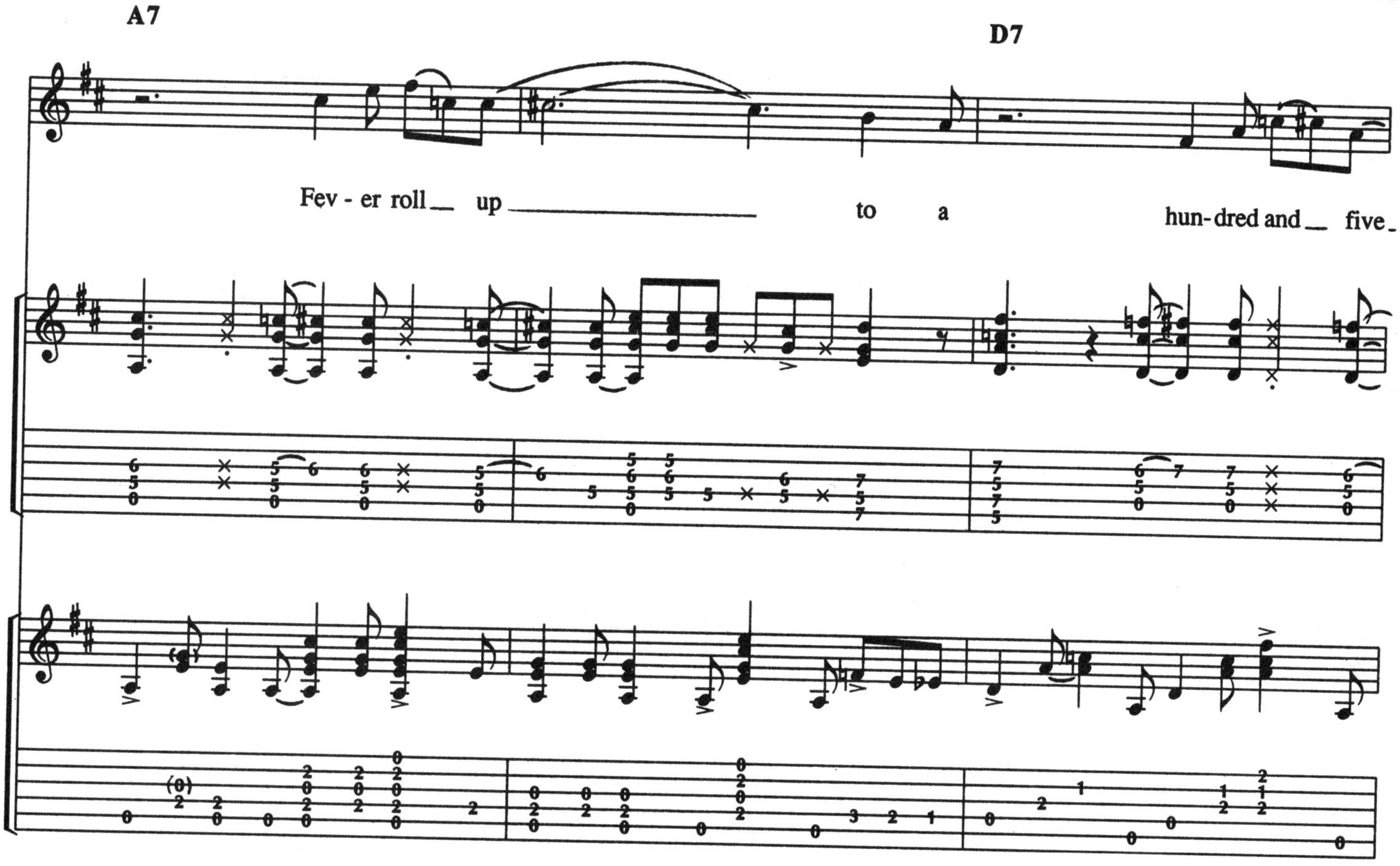
A7
D7
Fev - er roll up to a hun-dred and five

A7
Roll on up, gon-na roll back

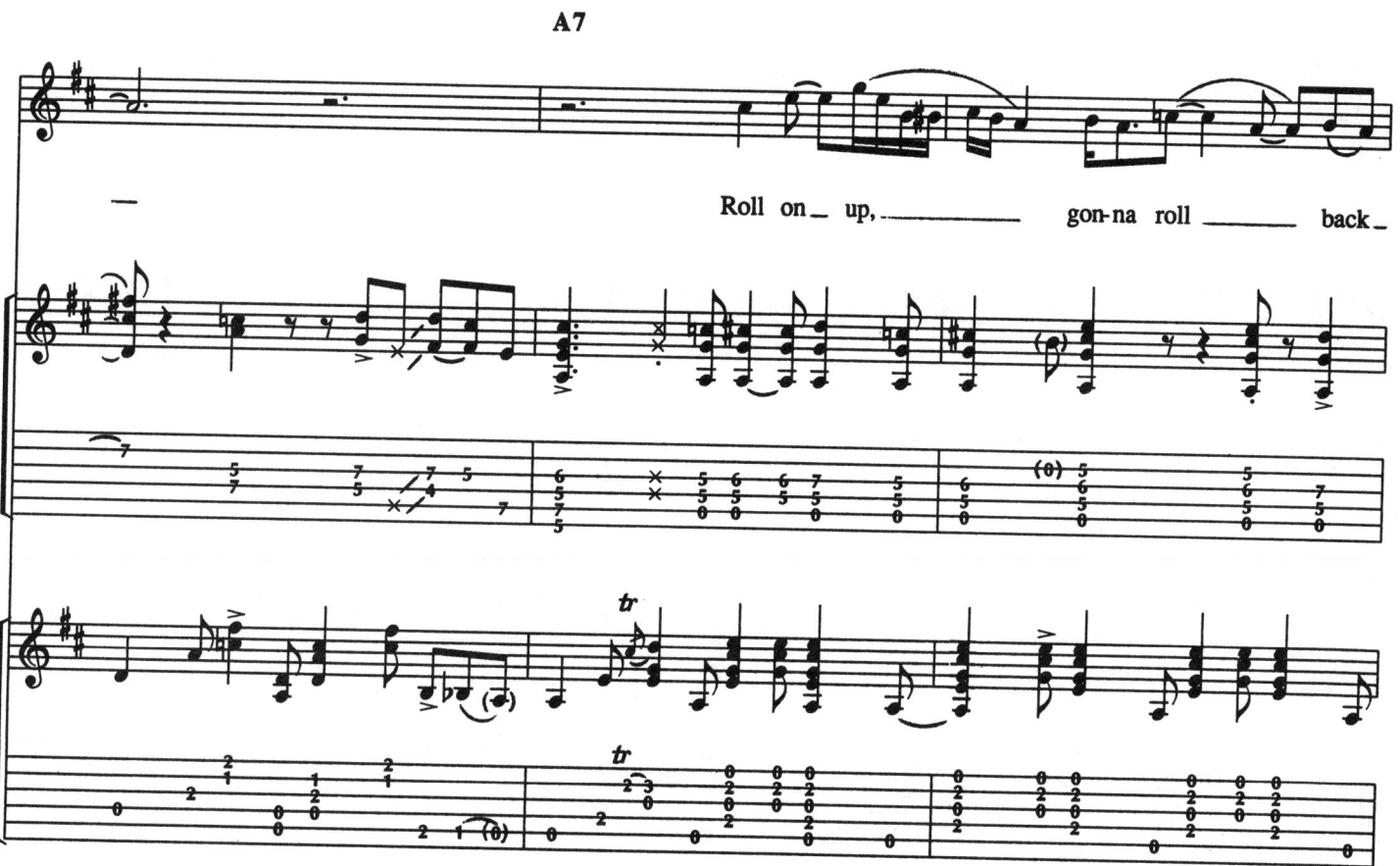

14

Lyrics:
See here_ how ev - 'ry thing lead up_ to_ this day,_ and it's just like_ an - y oth - er day_____ that's_

Em
D5
Dm
D
ev - er been.
Sun go - ing
mp
mf

G
C
Em
Am
up and then the sun go - ing down.
mp

Fmaj7
C
Shine thru my win- dow and my friends they come a -
mf
mp

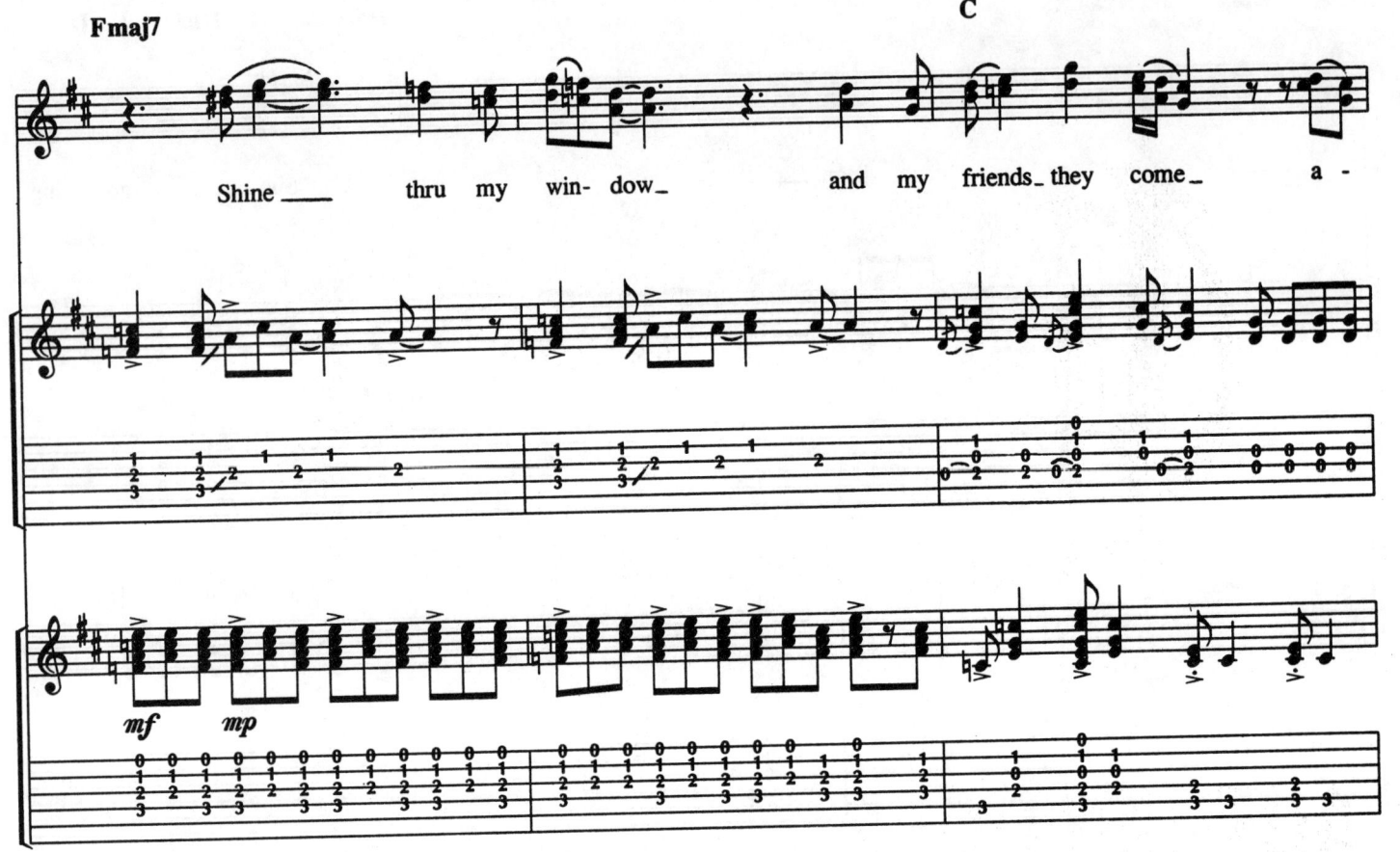

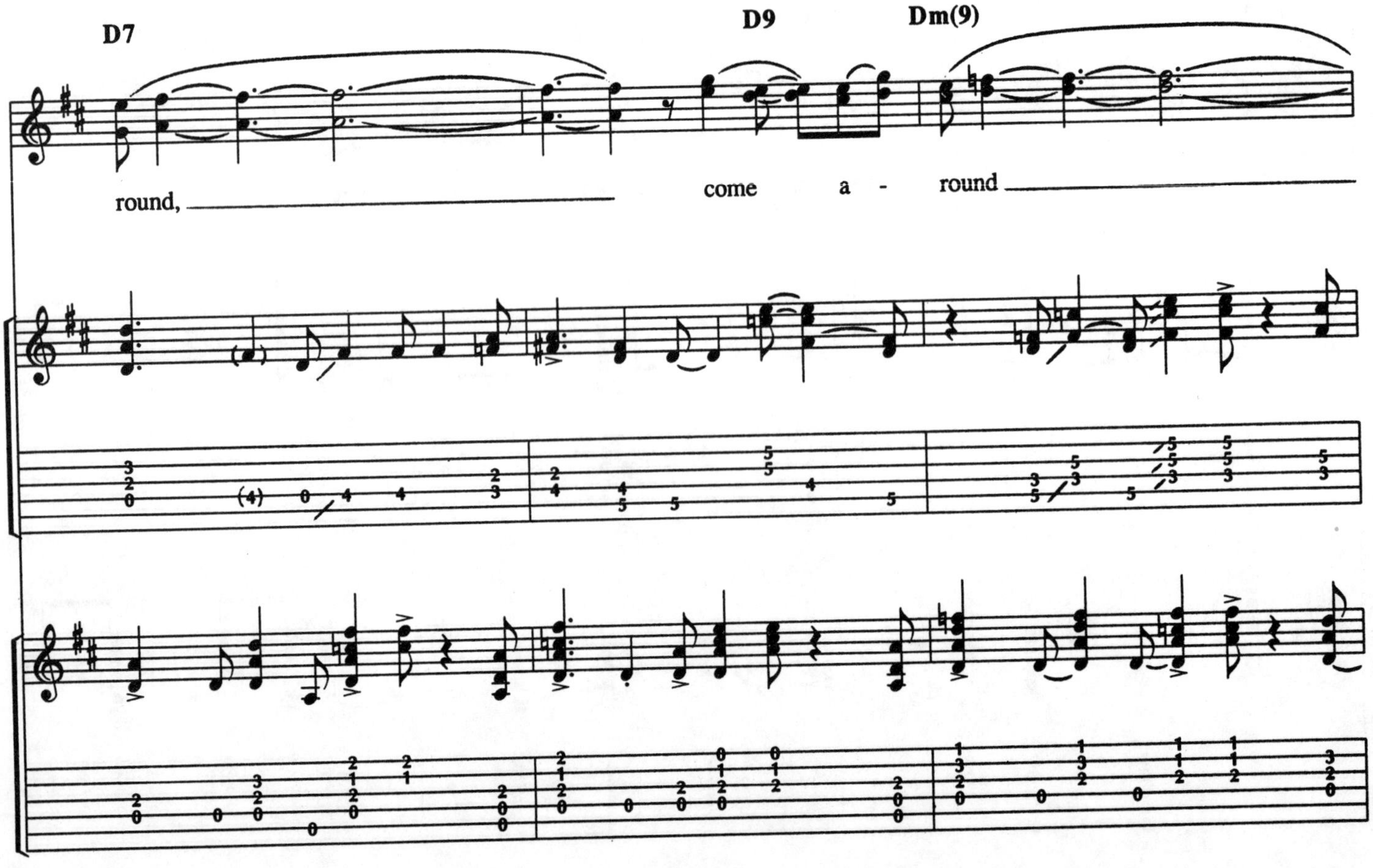
D7
D9
Dm(9)
round, come a - round

come a - round. Ah.

Verse 4:

A7   D7

The peo-ple may know,   but the peo-ple don't care

A7

that a man can be as poor as

me. Take a look at poor Pe-ter;___ he's_ ly - ing in pain.___

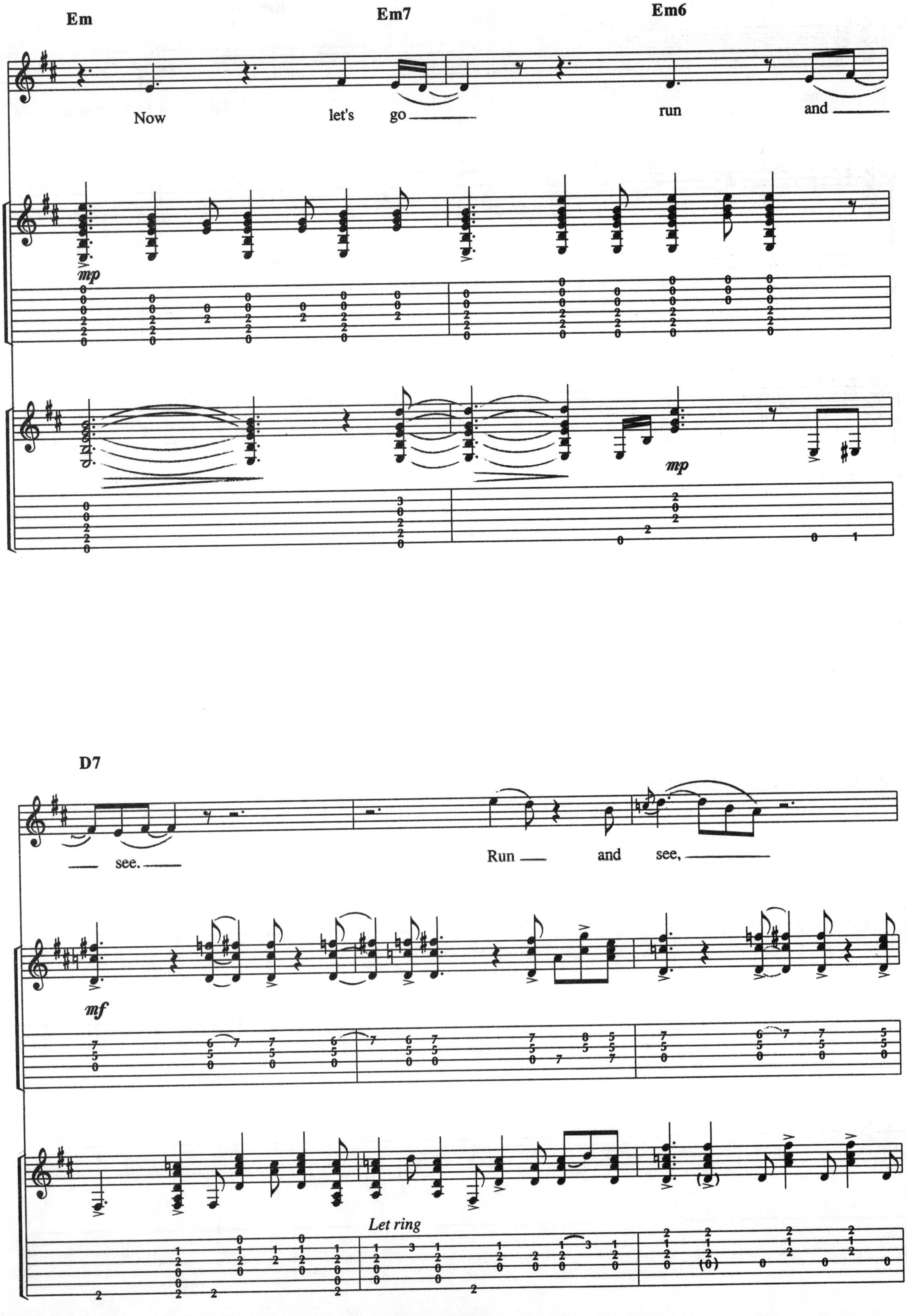
Em
Em7
Em6
Now
let's
go
run
and
mp
D7
see.
Run
and
see,
mf
Let ring

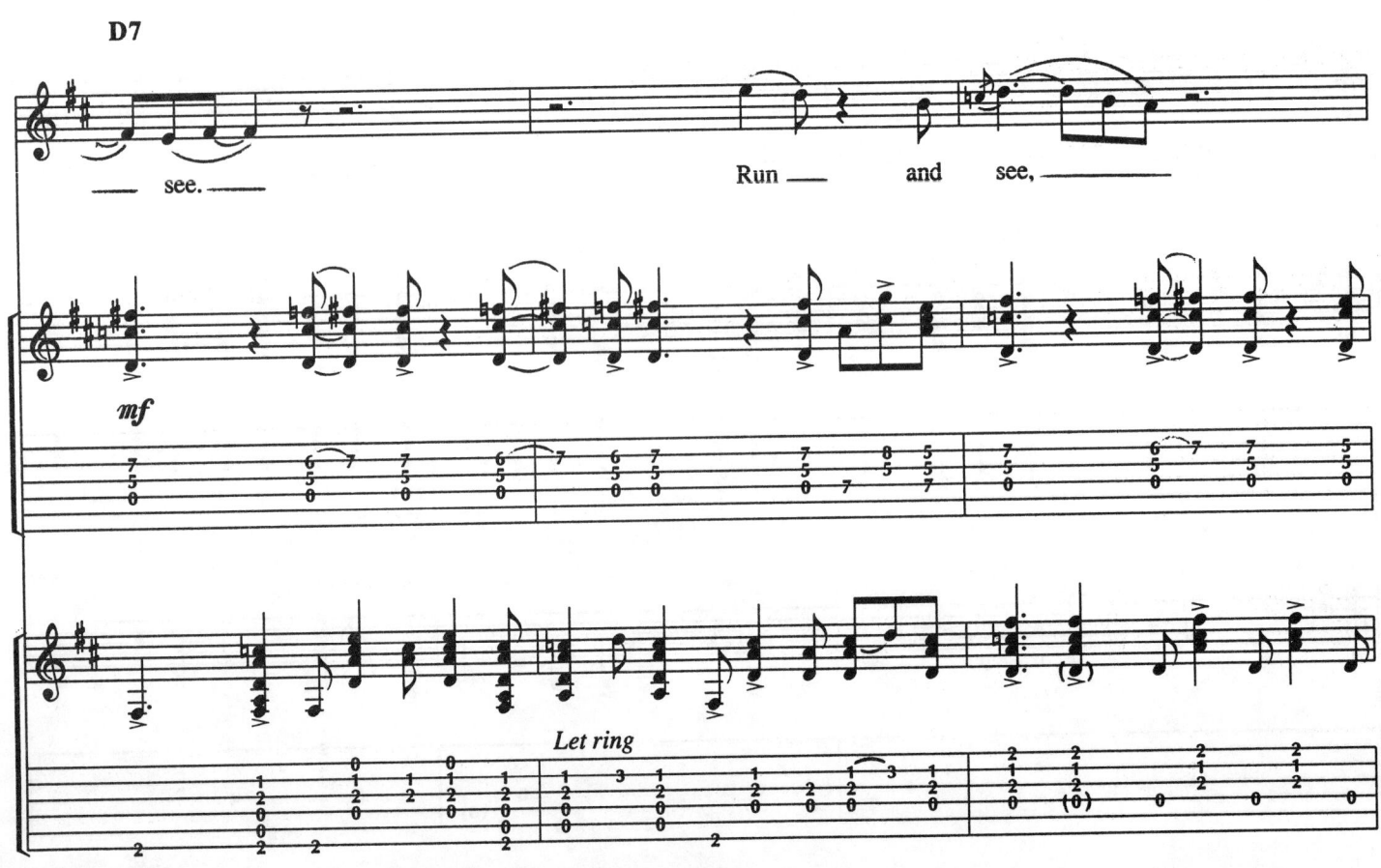

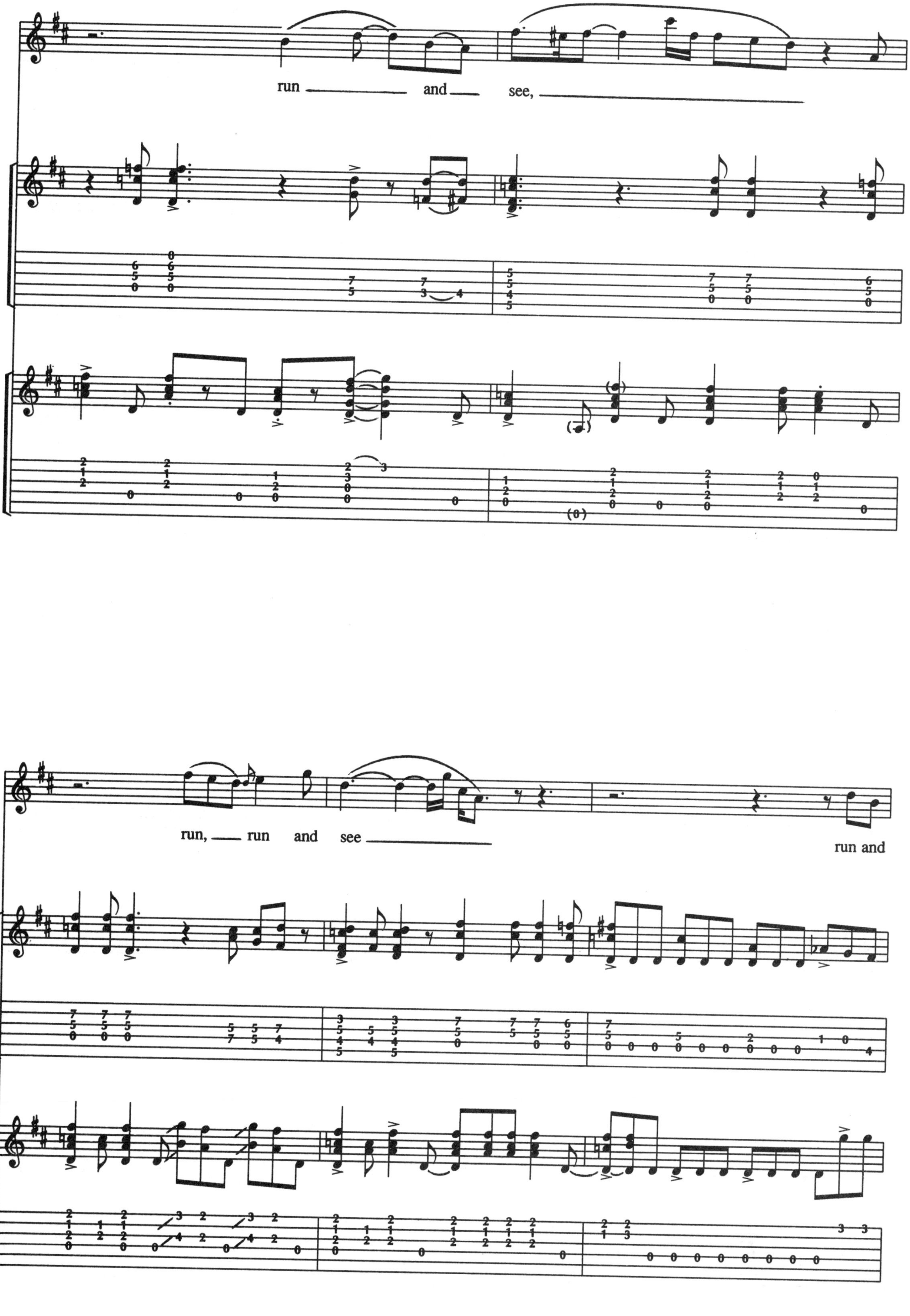
run and see,
run, run and see
run and

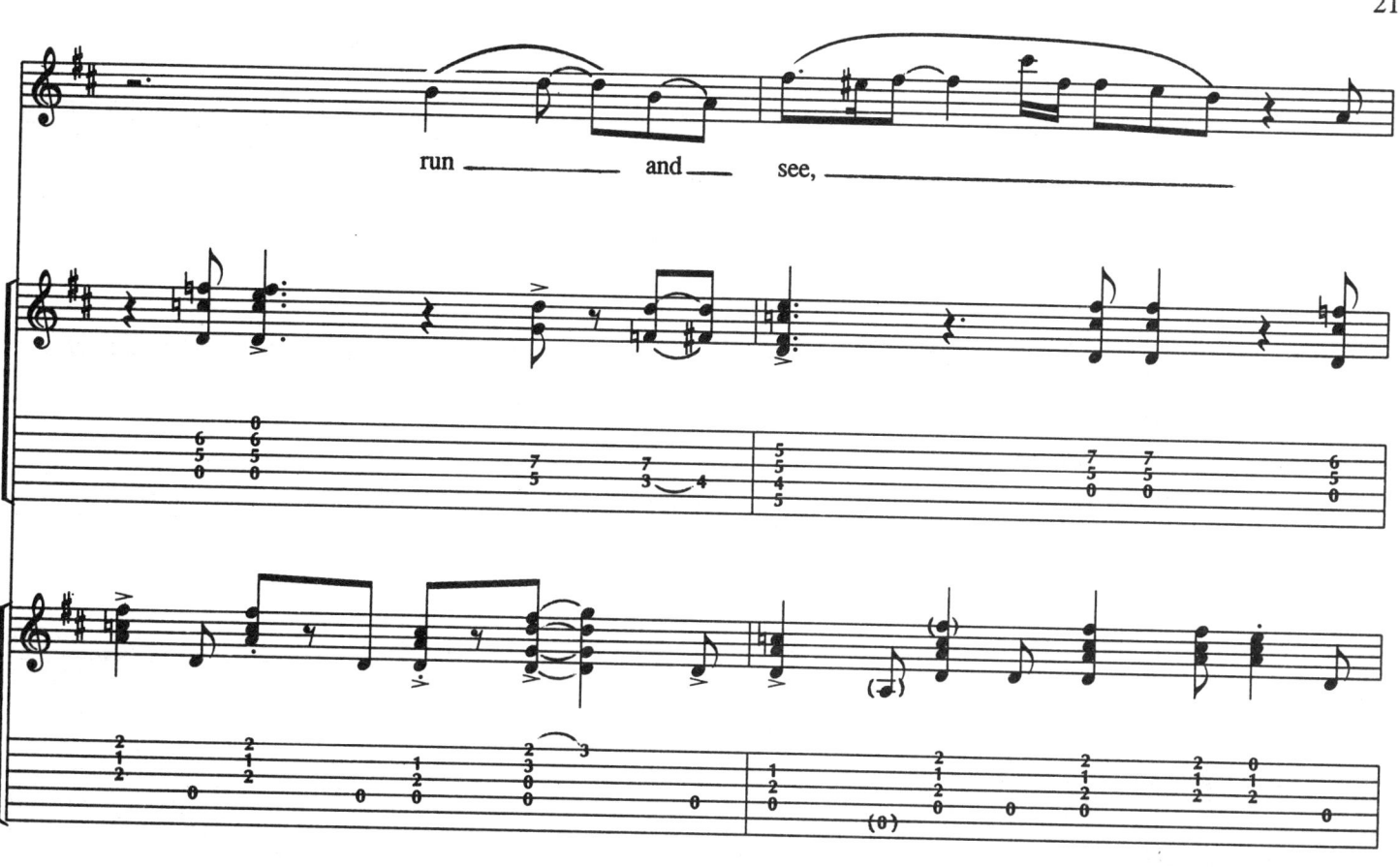

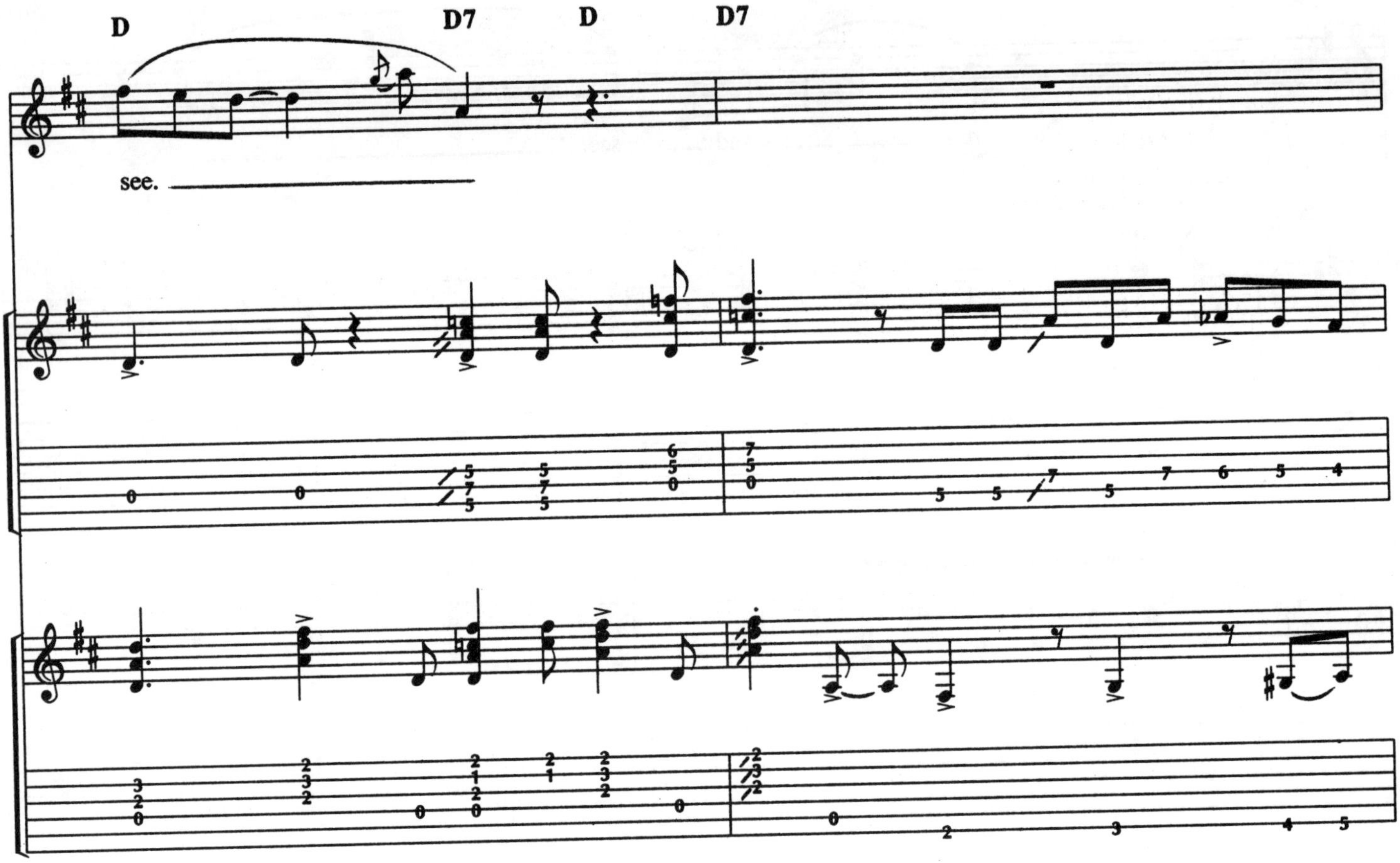
D
D7
D
D7
see.

ritard.
ritard.

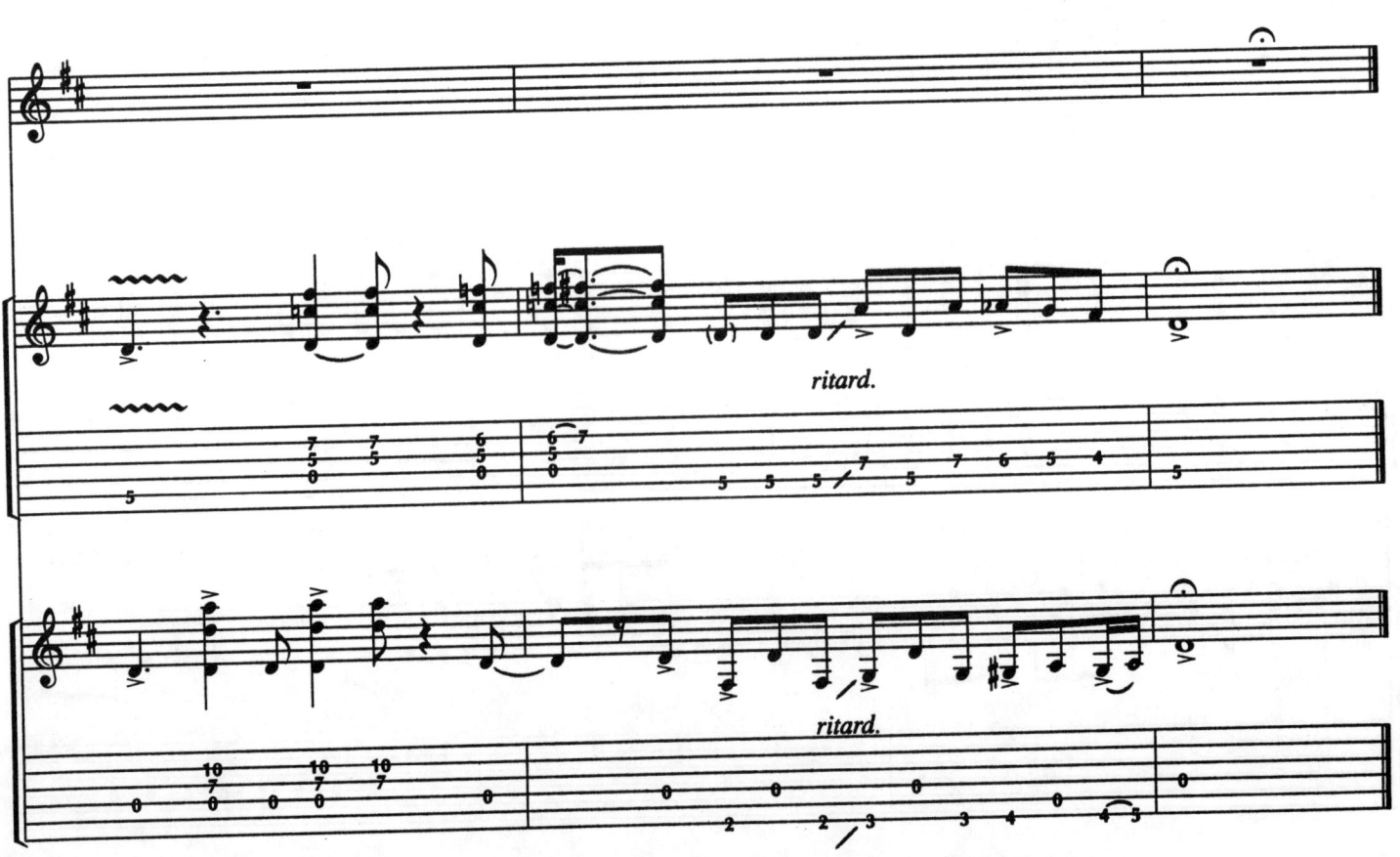

BOX OF RAIN

Words by
ROBERT HUNTER

Music by
PHILIP LESH

© 1970, 1991 ICE NINE PUBLISHING CO., INC.

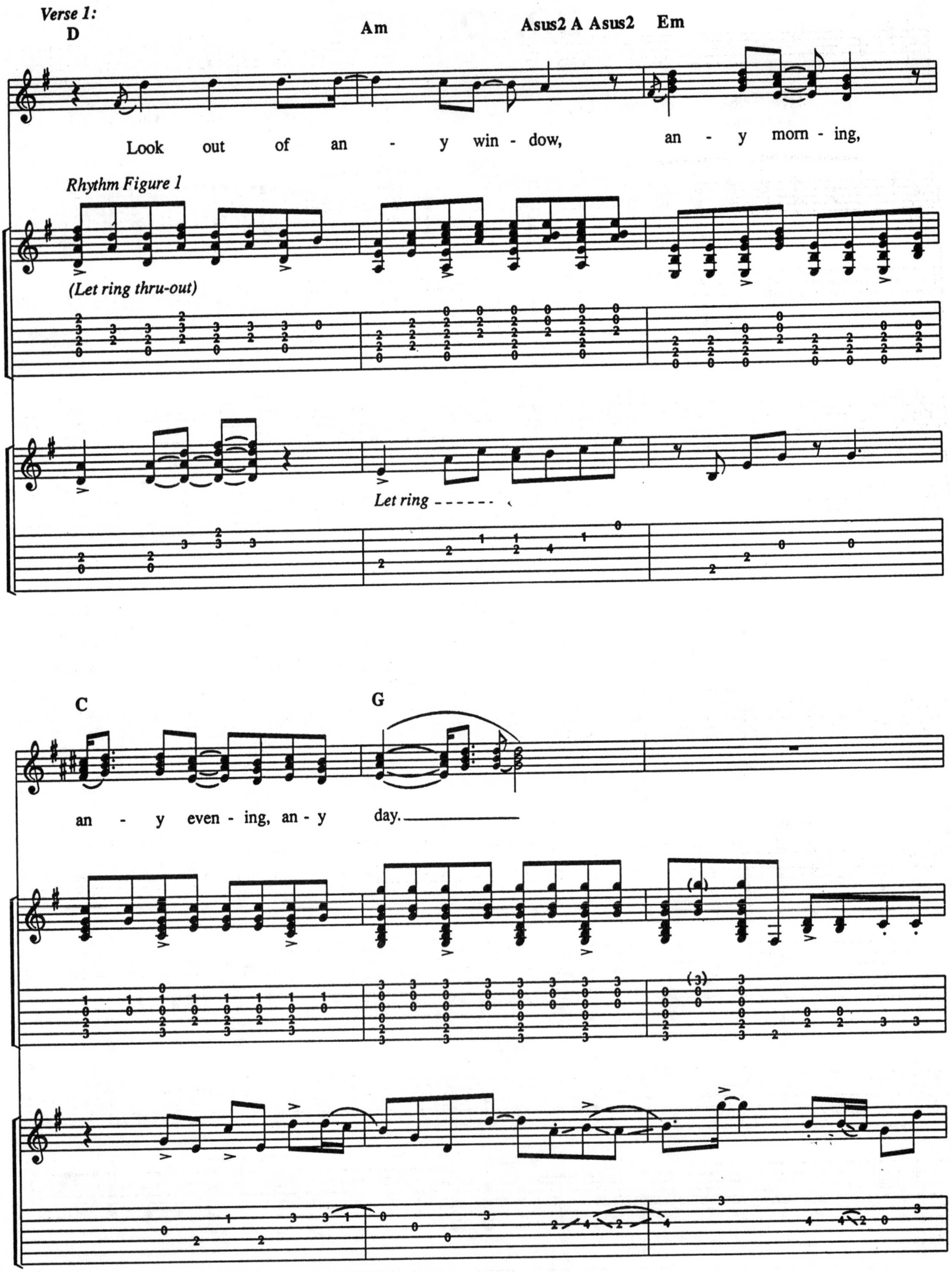
Verse 1:
D
Am
Asus2 A Asus2
Em
Look out of an - y win - dow, an - y morn - ing,
Rhythm Figure 1
(Let ring thru-out)
Let ring
C
G
an - y even - ing, an - y day.

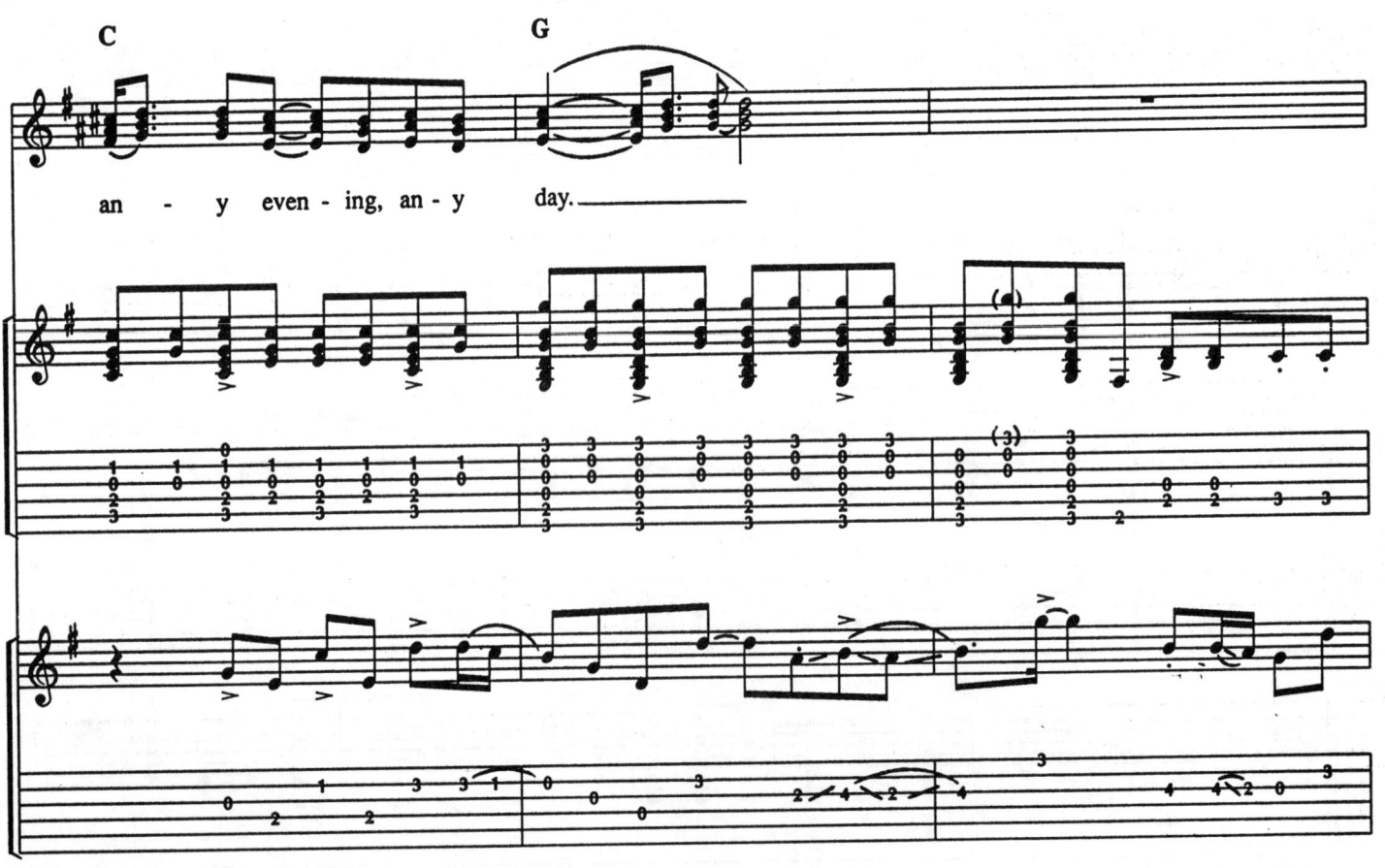

D
G
Am
Em
May - be the sun is shin - ing, birds are wing - ing, or
mp
mf
mp

G
Gsus2 G
A
Asus4 A
Asus2
Asus4 A
rain is fall - ing from a heav - y sky.
mf
mp

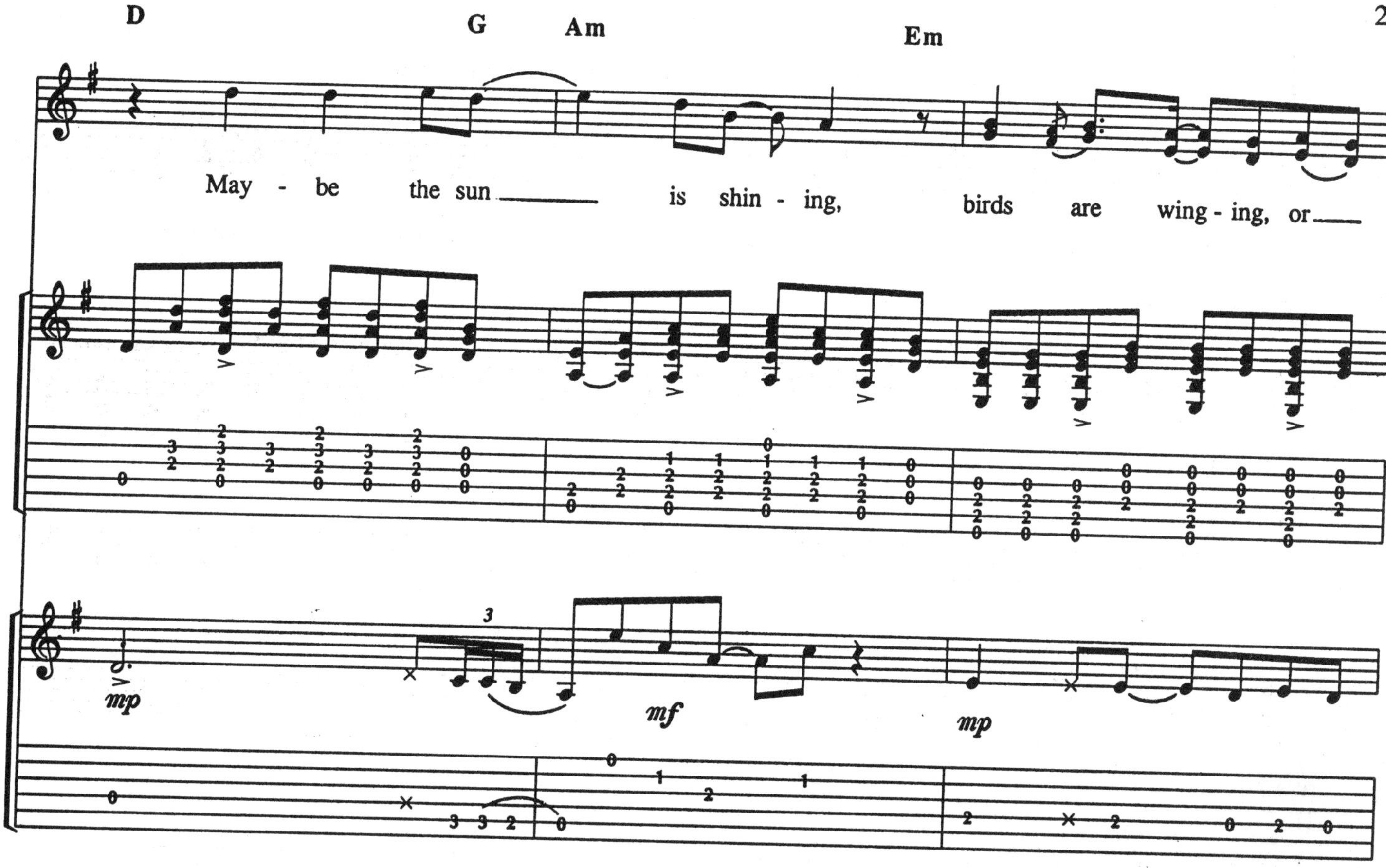

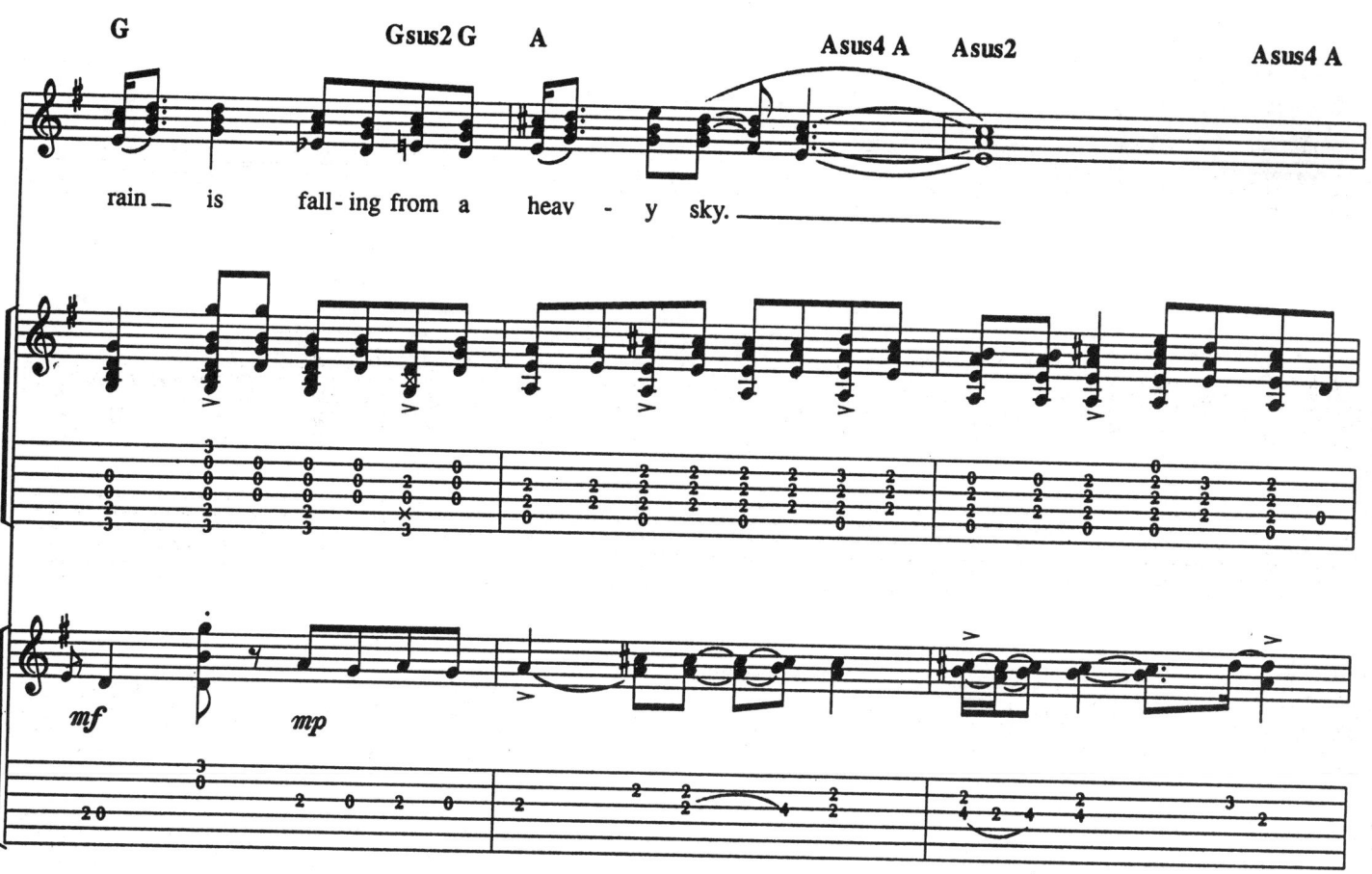

D
G
Am
Em
What — do you want — me to — do, — to do — for — you, — to
* (Hold bend)
+1

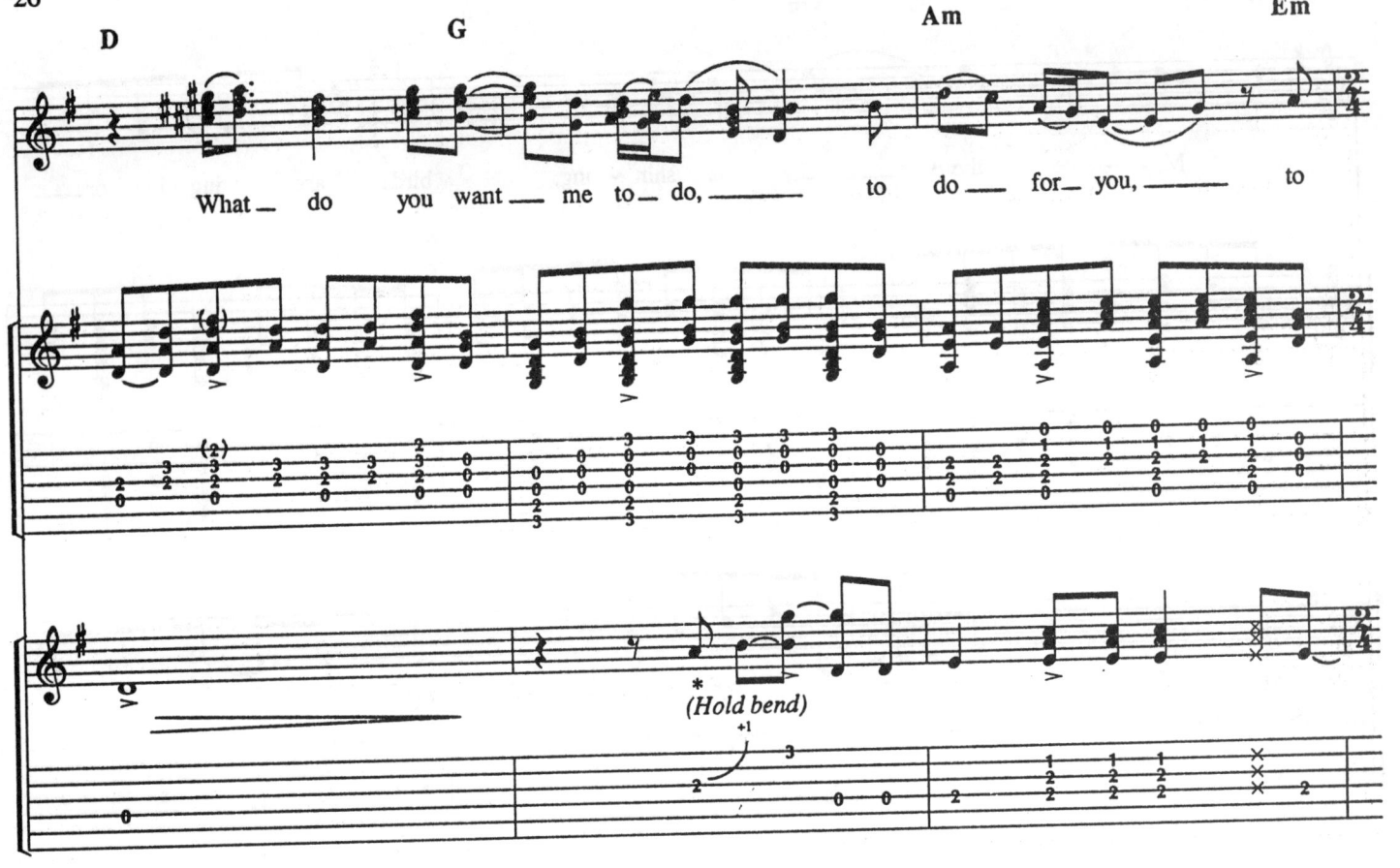

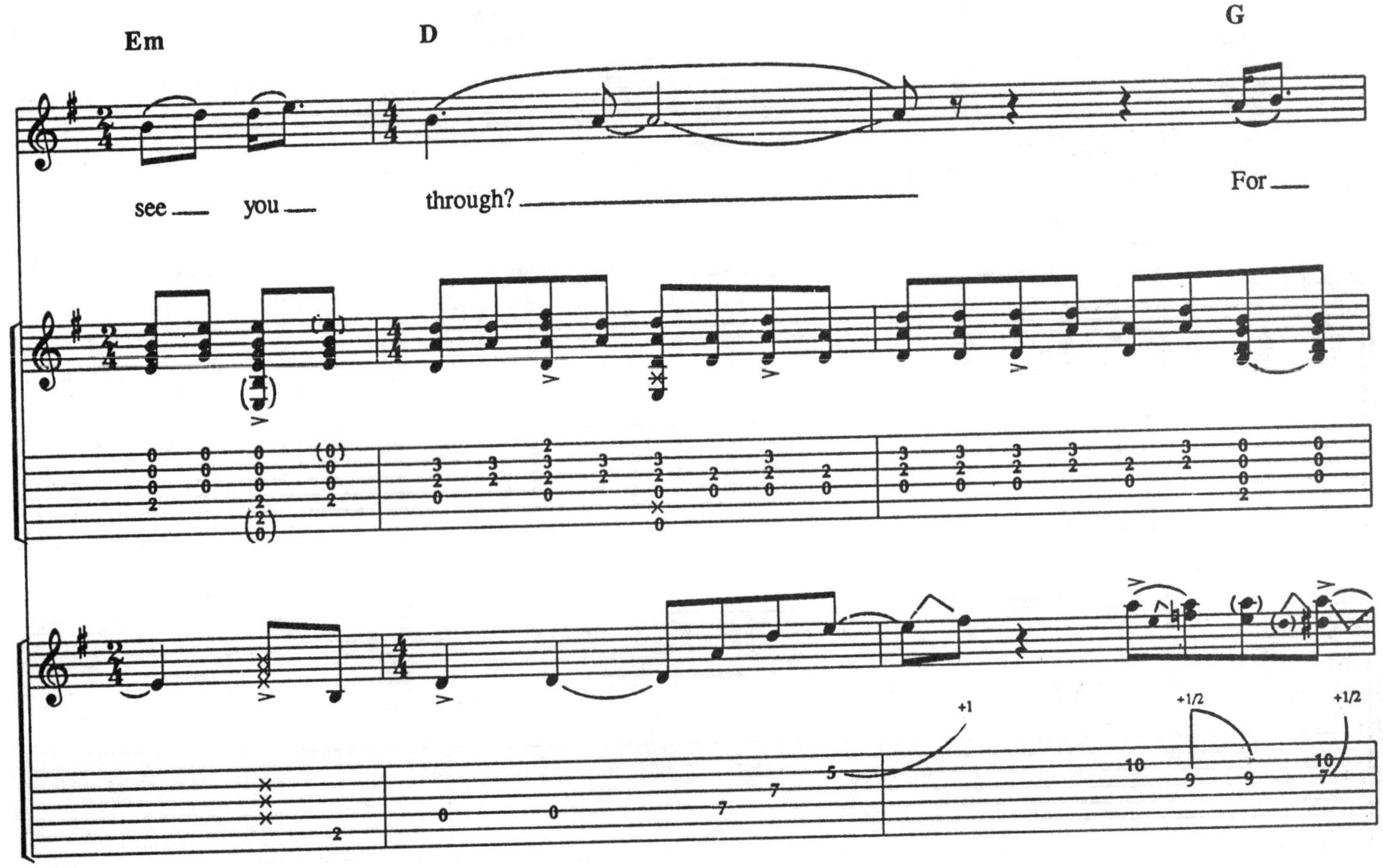
Em
D
G
see — you — through? —
For —
+1
+1/2
+1/2

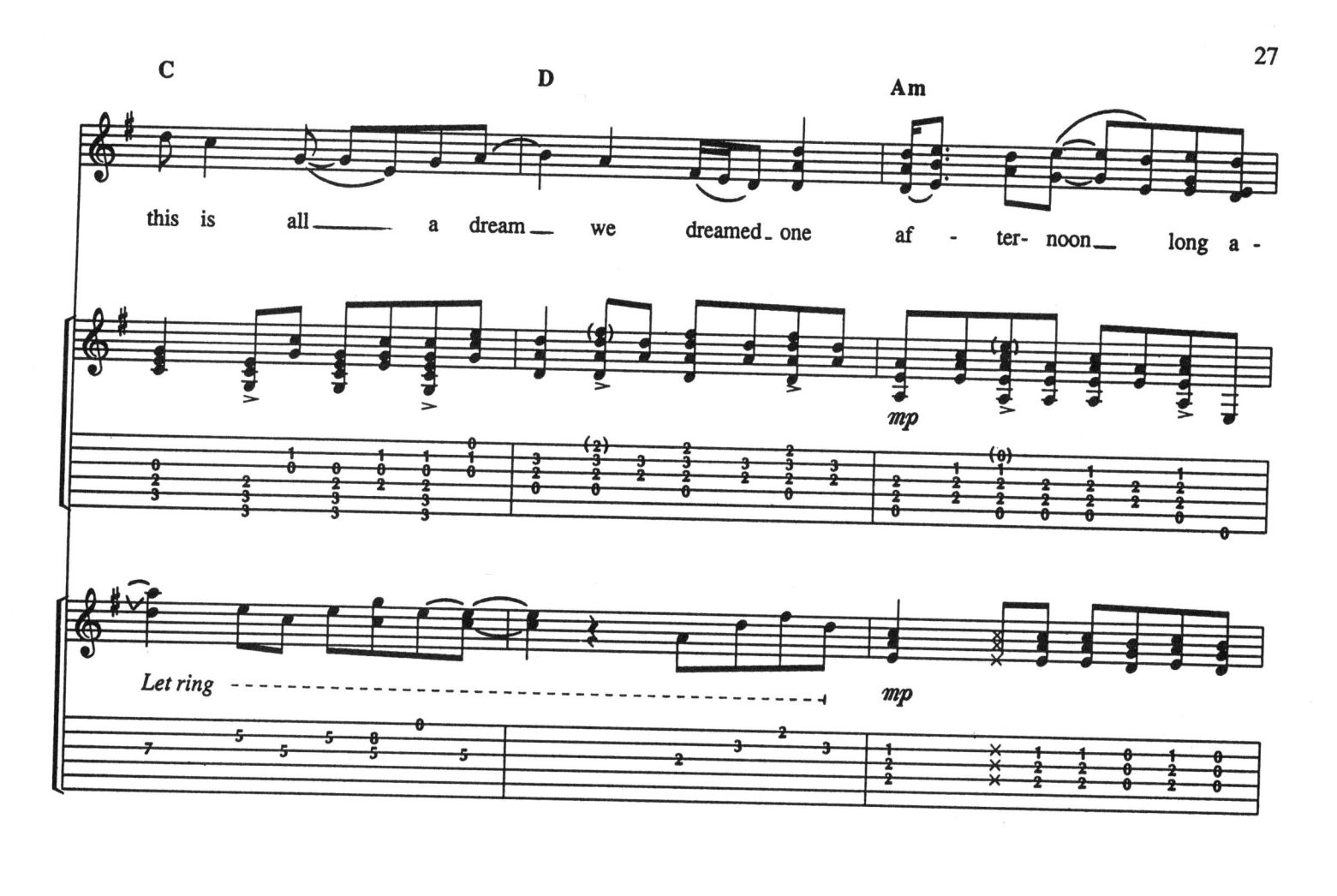

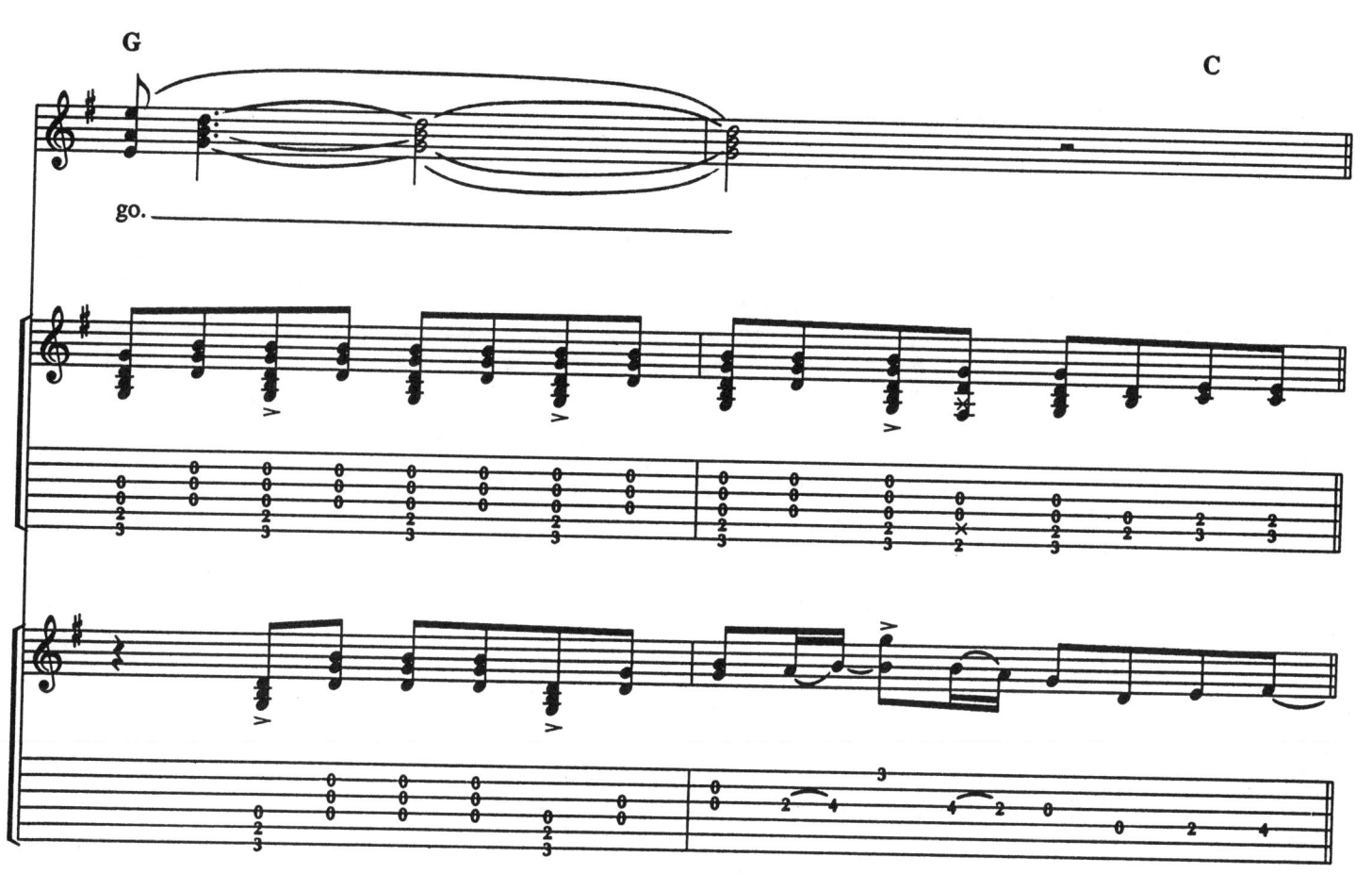

this is all ___ a dream ___ we dreamed ___ one af- ter- noon ___ long a-

go.

Verse 2:

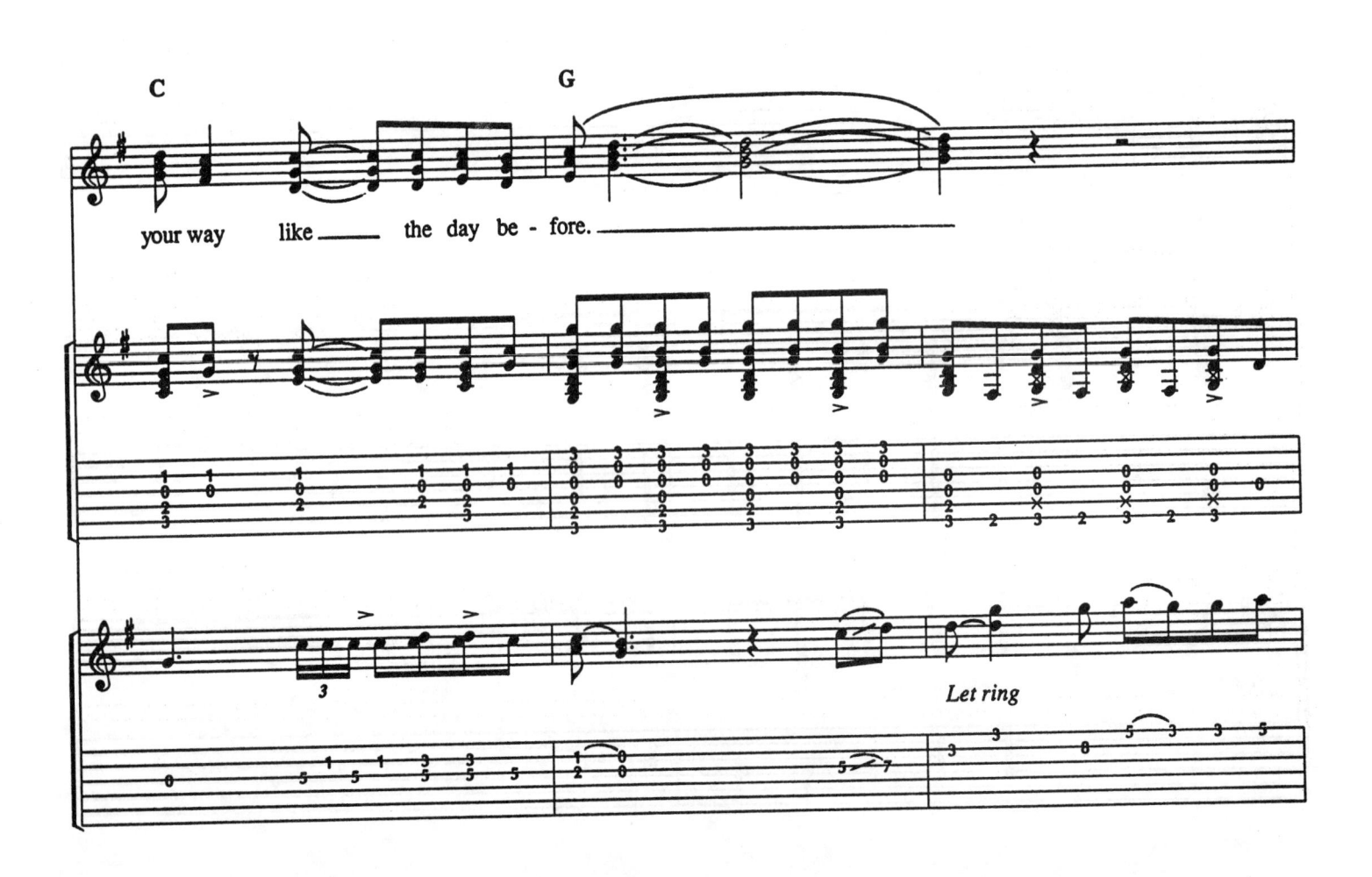

Walk out of an-y door-way, feel your way, feel your way like the day be-fore.

29

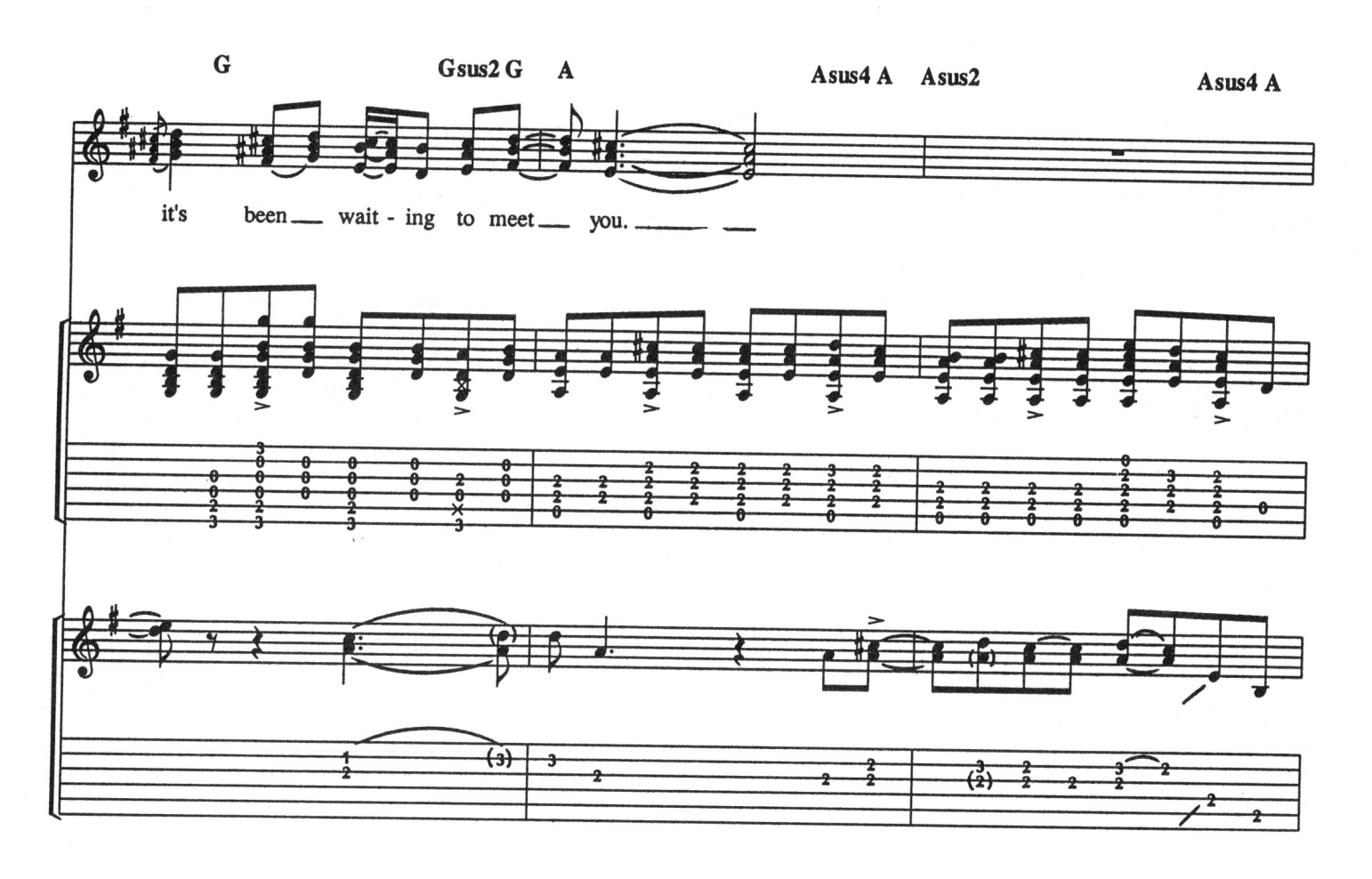

Maybe you'll find direction around some corner where it's been waiting to meet you.

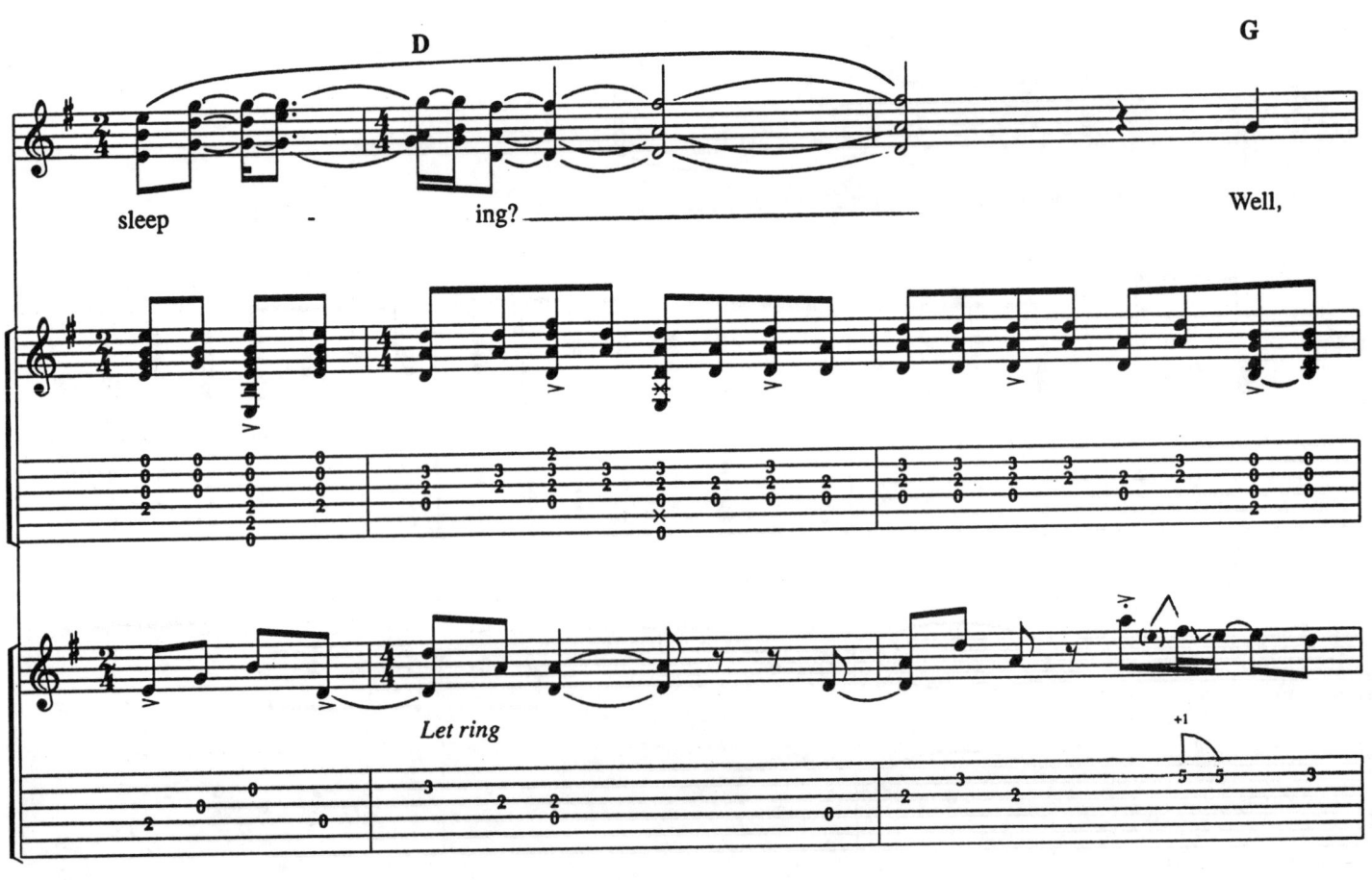

What do you want me to do, to watch for you while you're sleep-ing? Well,

Am
C
please don't be sur - prised when you find
mp
mp
Let ring
G
D
3
me dream - ing, too.
mp

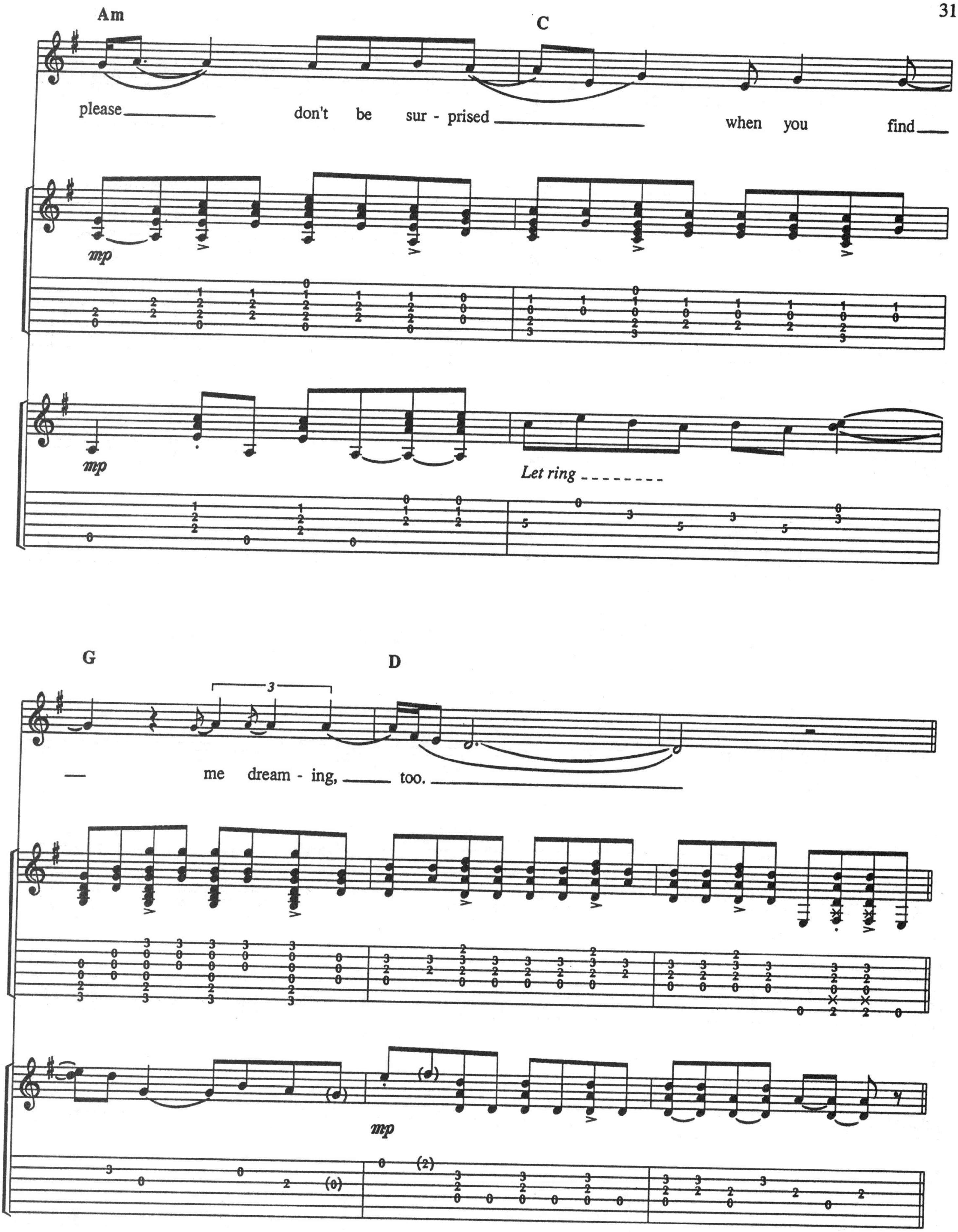

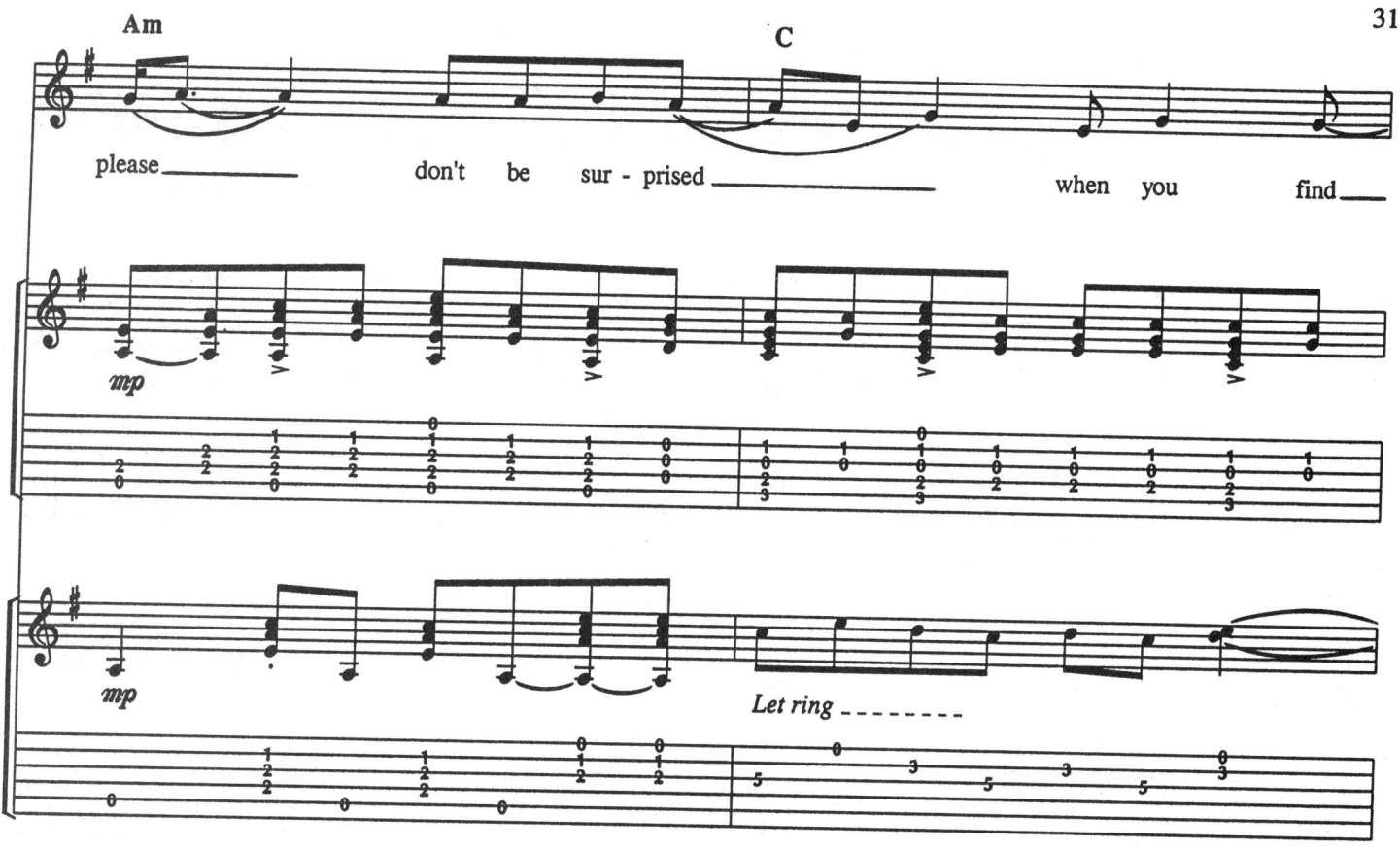

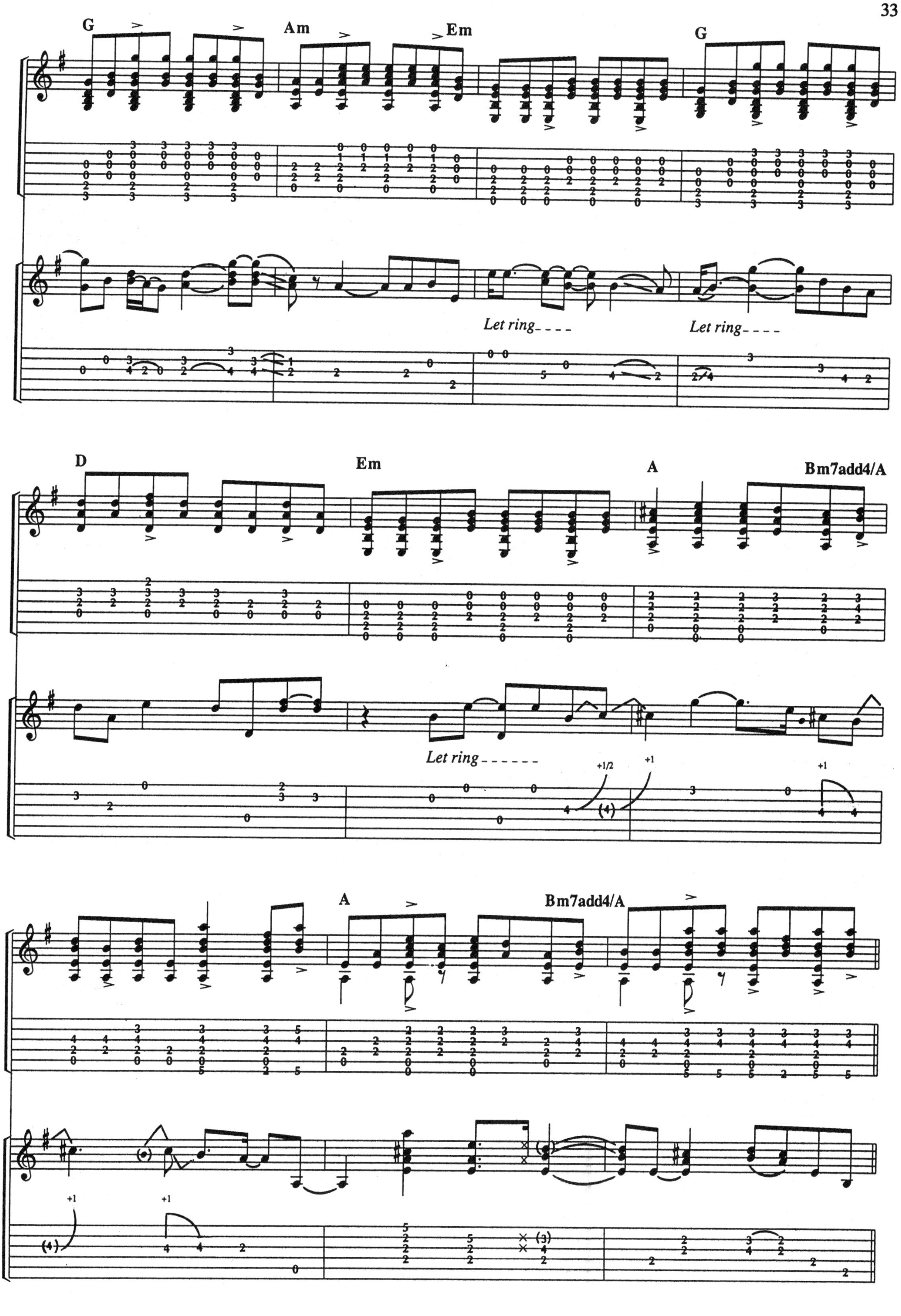
G
Am
Em
G
Let ring
Let ring
D
Em
A
Bm7add4/A
Let ring
A
Bm7add4/A

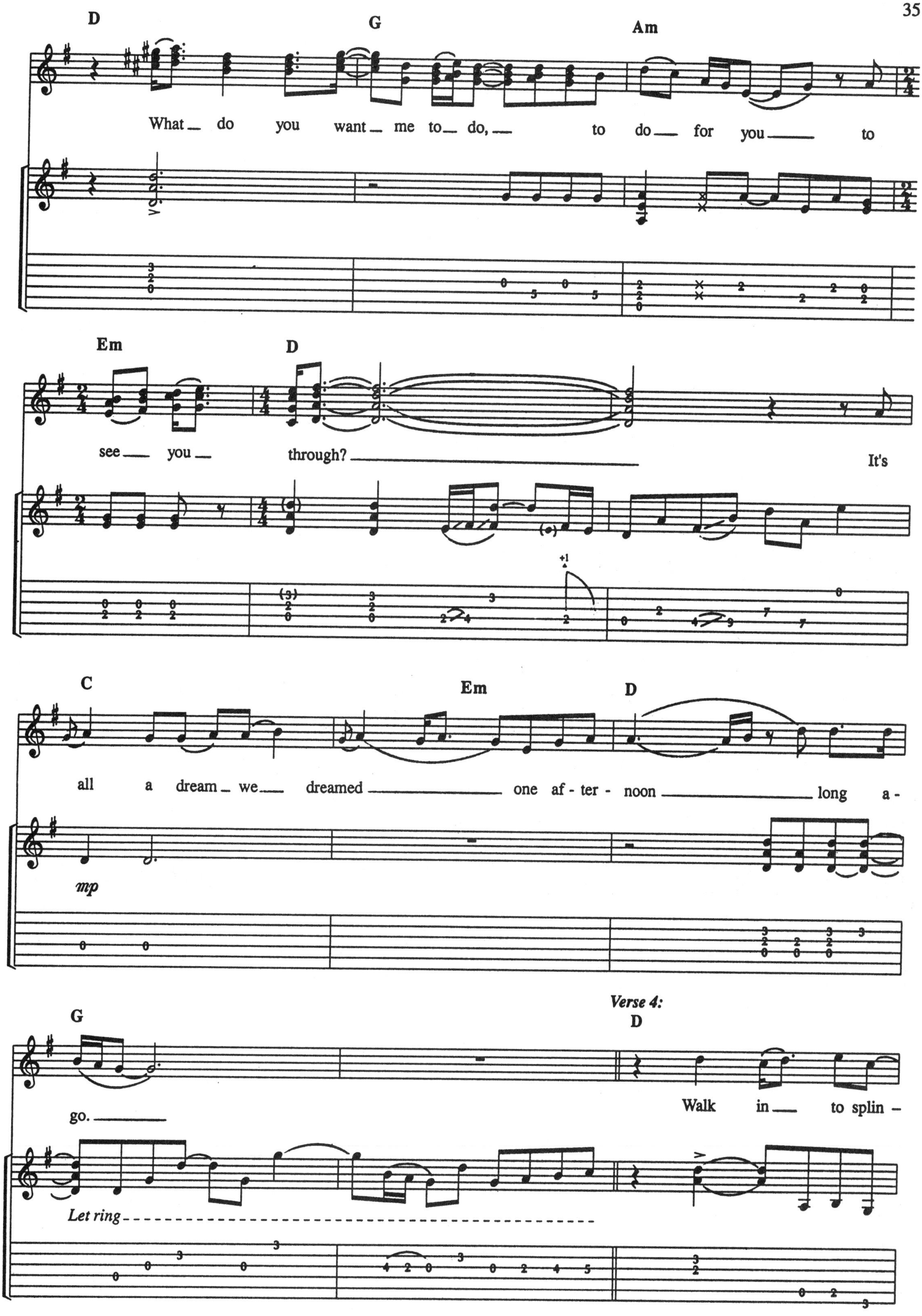
D
G
Am
What do you want me to do, to do for you to
Em
D
see you through?
It's
C
Em
D
all a dream we dreamed one af - ter - noon long a -
mp
G
Verse 4:
D
go.
Walk in to splin -
Let ring

G
Am
G
Em
me to do, to do for you to see you
D
Am
through? A box of rain will
Let ring
C/G
G
D
ease the pain and love will see you through.
Bridge:
G
Am
G Am G
Just a box of rain, wind and
Let ring

38

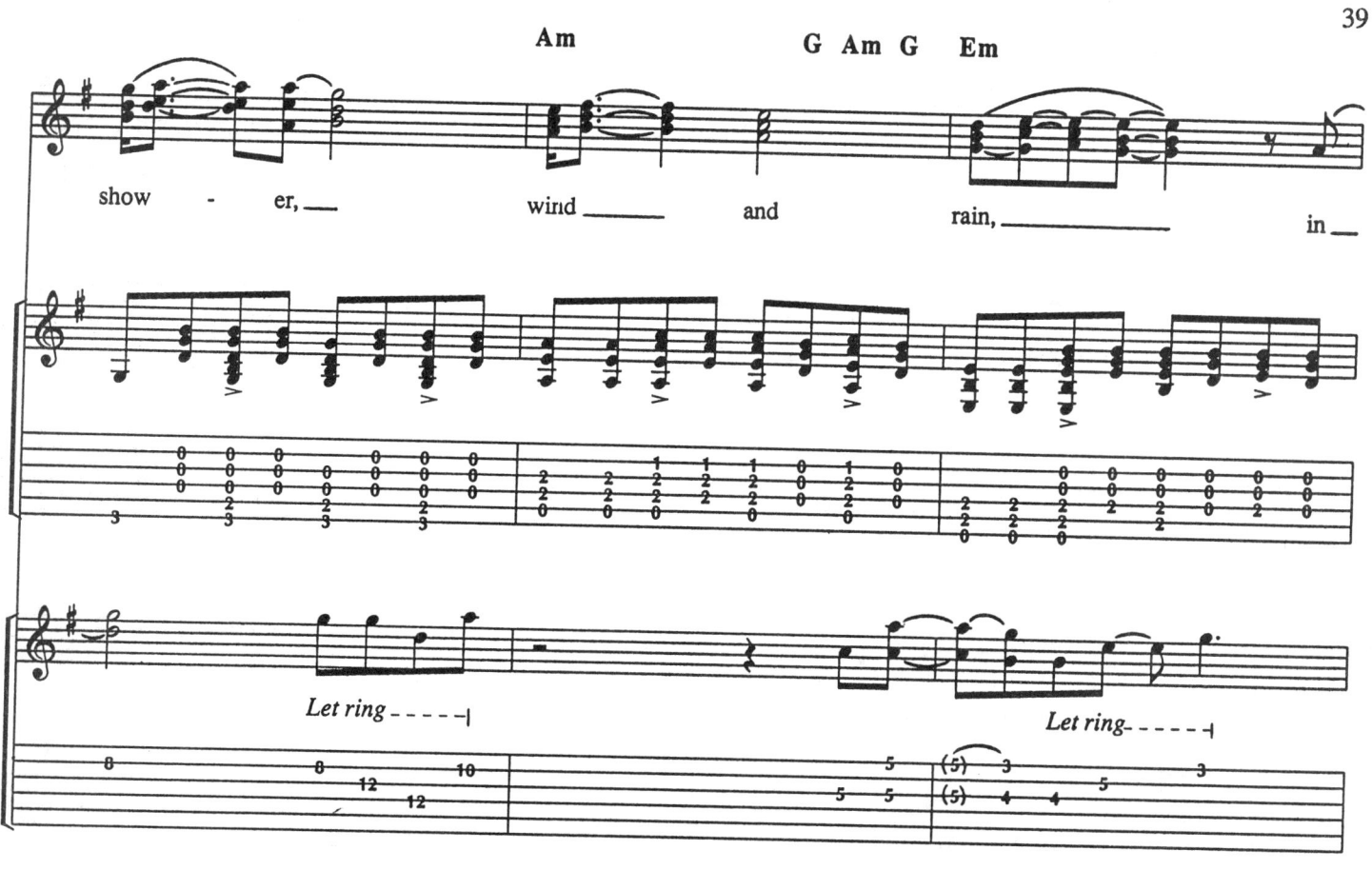

shower, wind and rain, in and out the window like a moth before a

40

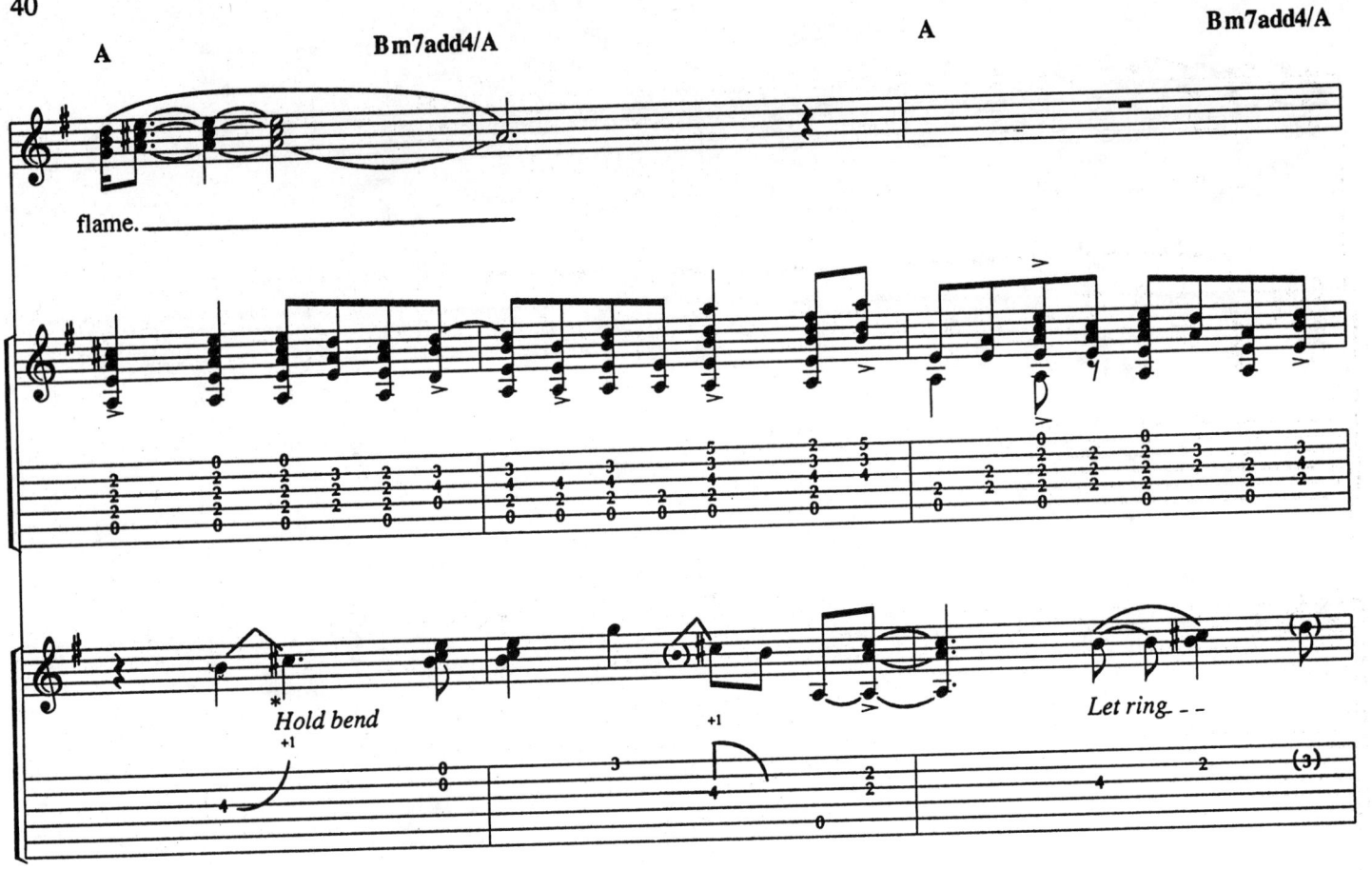

| A | Bm7add4/A | A | Bm7add4/A |

flame.

*Hold bend +1 Let ring

Chorus:
D   Em

And it's   just a box of rain;   I don't know

41

who put it there; be - lieve it if you need it

or leave it if you dare.

Let ring

Gradual bend
+1/2

42

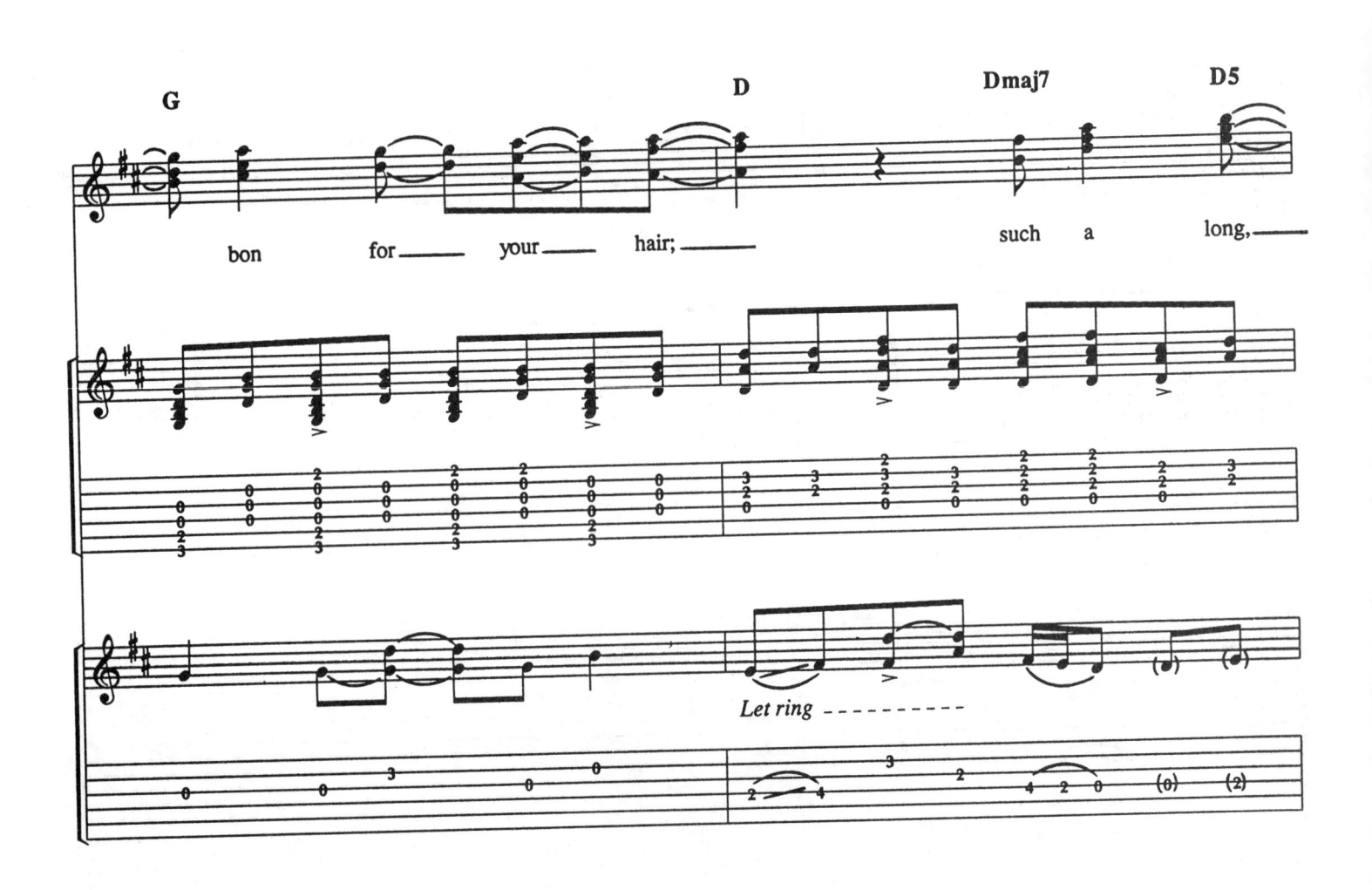

And it's just a box of rain, or a rib-bon for your hair; such a long,

long time to be gone and a short time to be there.

CASEY JONES

Words by ROBERT HUNTER
Music by JERRY GARCIA

Medium tempo

Chorus:

Driv-in' that train, high on co-caine, Ca-sey Jones, you'd bet-ter watch your speed.

*Two Guitars arranged as one.

© 1970, 1991 ICE NINE PUBLISHING CO., INC.
All Rights Reserved

Trou-ble a - head, trou-ble be - hind, and you know that no-tion just crossed my mind.

Verse 1:
C
D
F
This old en - gine makes it on time.
leaves cen - tral sta - tion 'bout a
div.
G
C
quar - ter to nine.
Hits riv - er junc - tion at
div.
(Let ring)
mf

sev - en - teen to ___ at a quar - ter to ten ___ you know ___ it's trav-'lin' a - gain ___

Chorus:
Driv-in' that train ___ high on co-caine, ___ Ca - sey Jones ___ you'd bet - ter

watch your speed. Trou-ble a-head, trou-ble be-hind,

and you know that no-tion just crossed my mind.

Verse 2:

Trou-ble a-head the ___ la-dy in red, ___ take my ad-vice, ___ you'd ___ be bet-ter off ___ dead. ___ Switch-man's ___ sleep-ing train

50

| D | F | E7 | Am | G |

hun-dred and two___ is on the wrong track__ and__ head-ed for you.___

div.

Chorus:

| C | F |

Driv-in' that train,___ high on co- caine,___ Ca-sey Jones you'd bet-ter watch your speed. Trouble a-head, trouble be-hind, and you know that notion just crossed my mind.

52

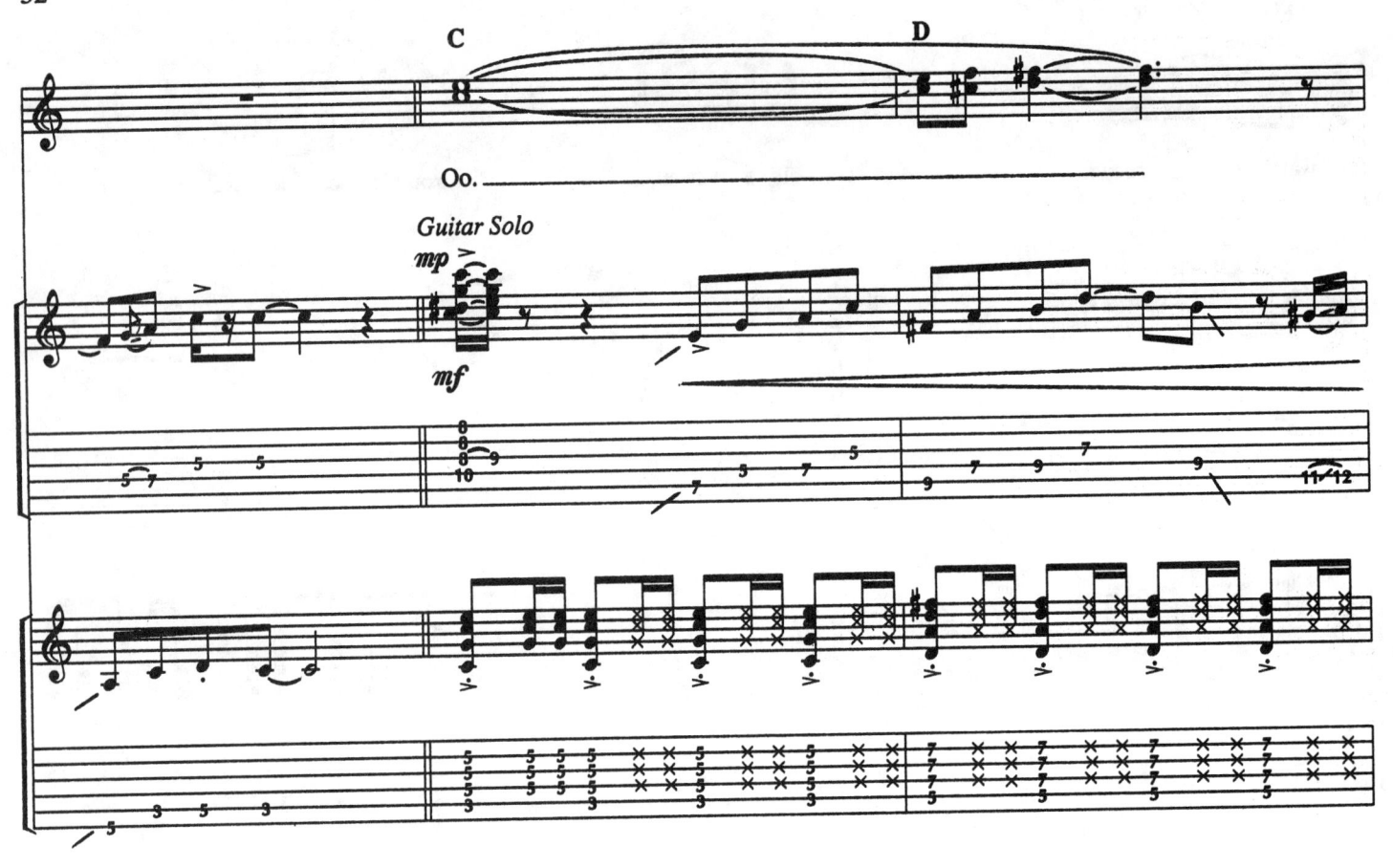

53

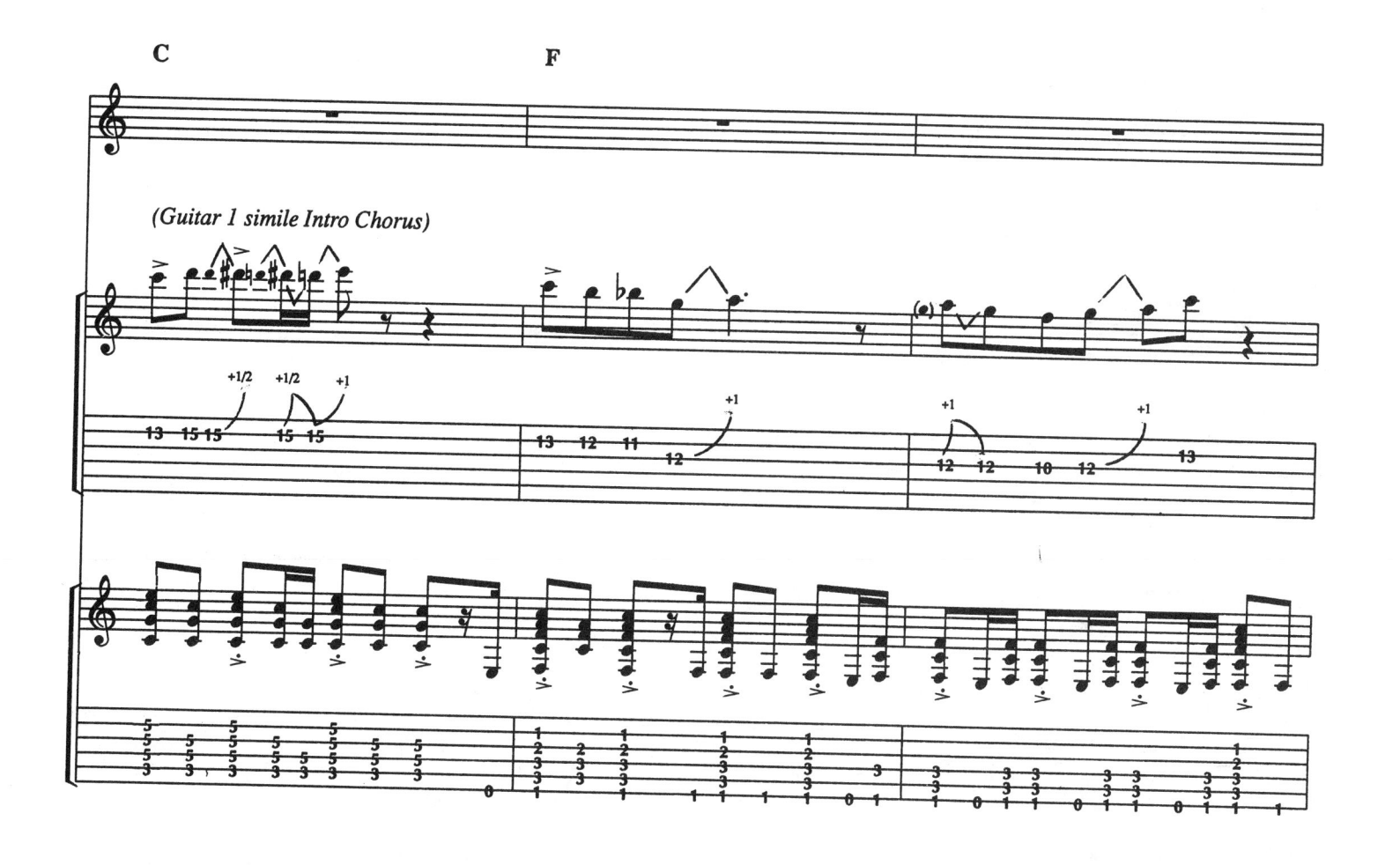

Drive your train. Hoo!

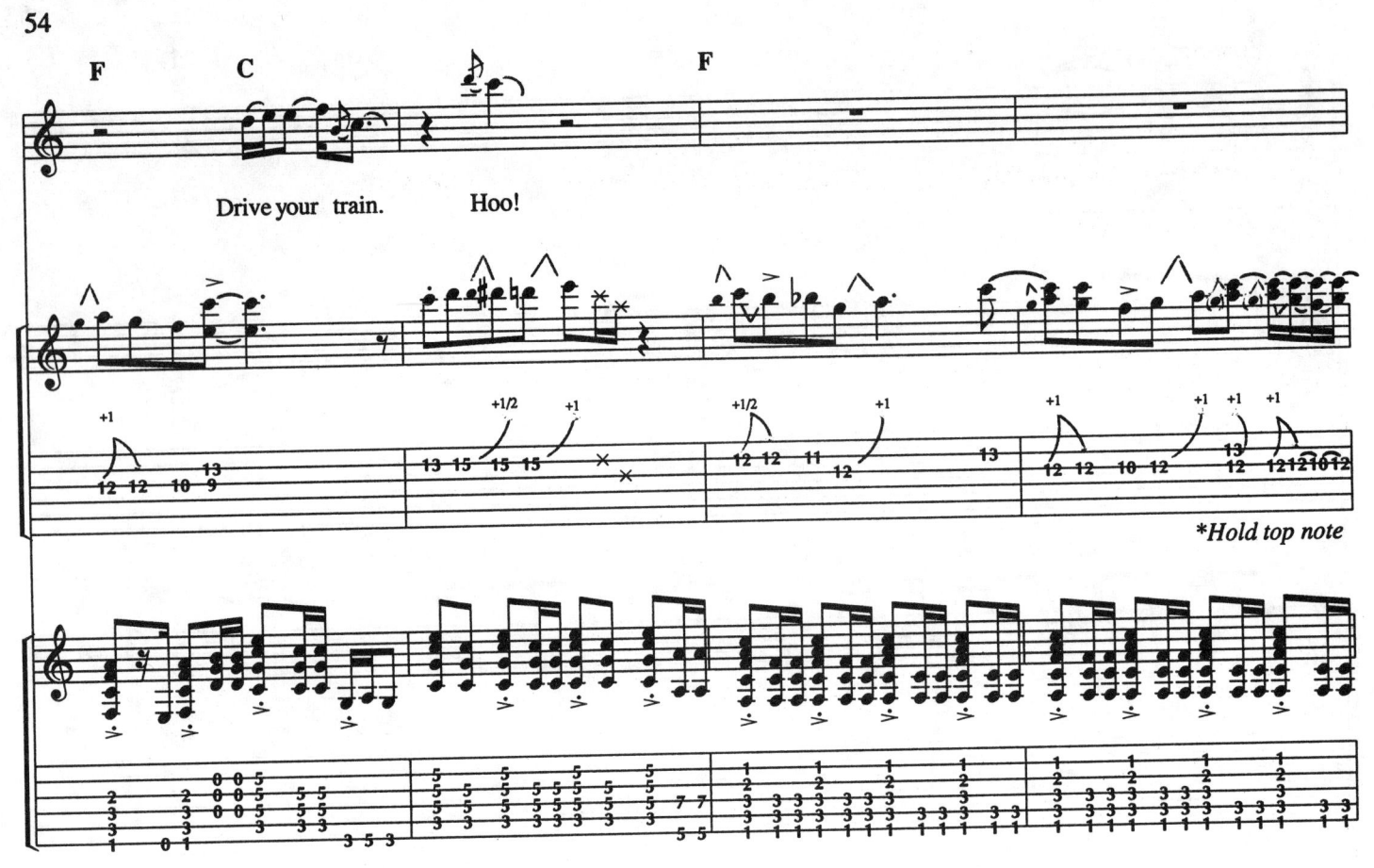

Verse 3:

Trou-ble with you is the trou-ble with me; got two good eyes but we still don't see. Come 'round the bend, you

56

D.S. 𝄋 al Coda ⊕

know it's the end. The fire man screams and the en-gine just gleams.

Coda
⊕

Driv-in' that train, high on co-caine,

57

Ca-sey Jones, you'd bet-ter watch your speed. Trouble a-head, trou-ble be-hind, and you know that no-tion just crossed my mind.

Driv-in' that train, high on co-caine, Ca - sey Jones you'd bet - ter watch your speed. Trou - ble a - head (You know) trou - ble be- hind, and

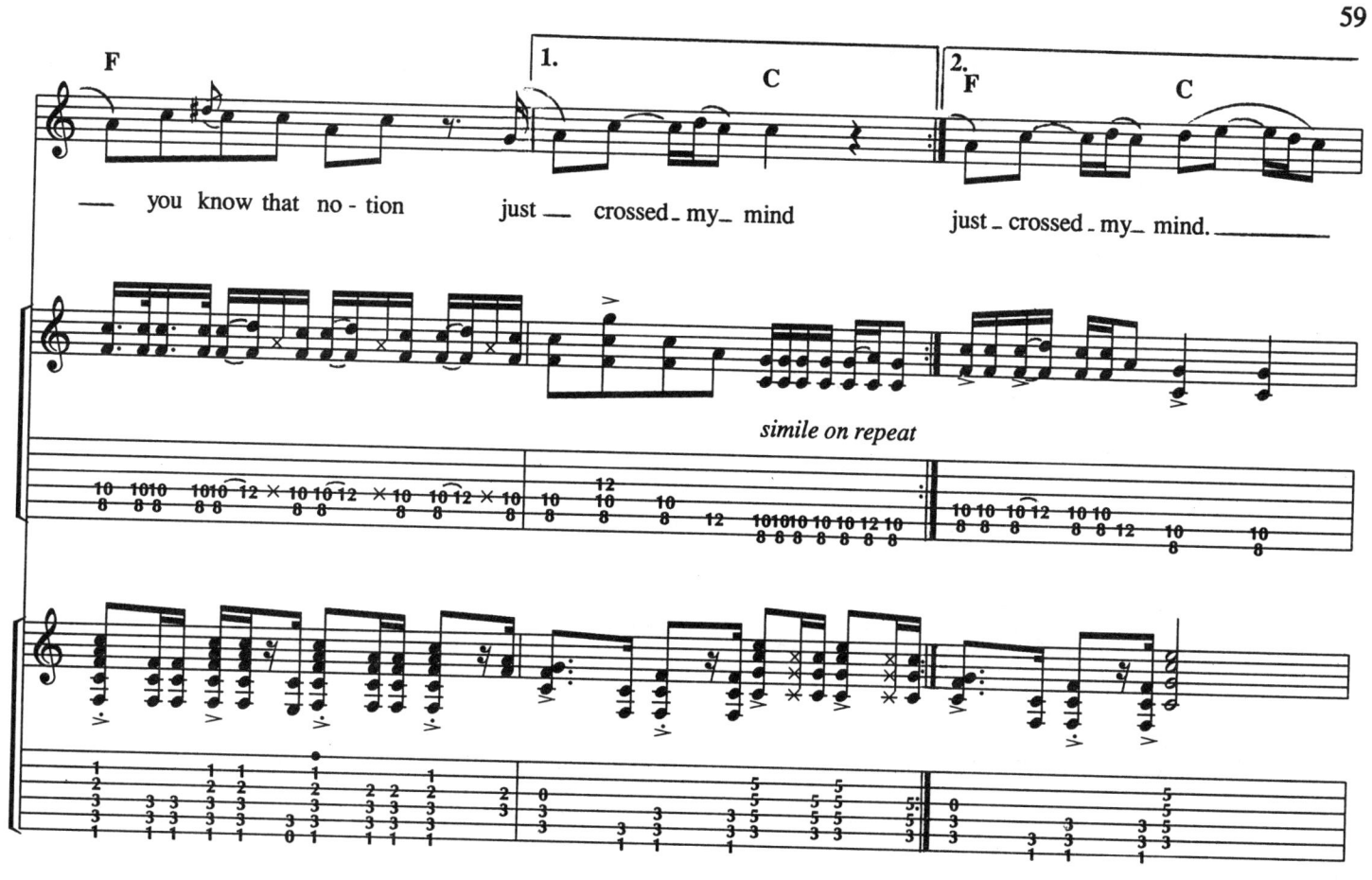

— you know that no-tion just — crossed my mind

simile on repeat

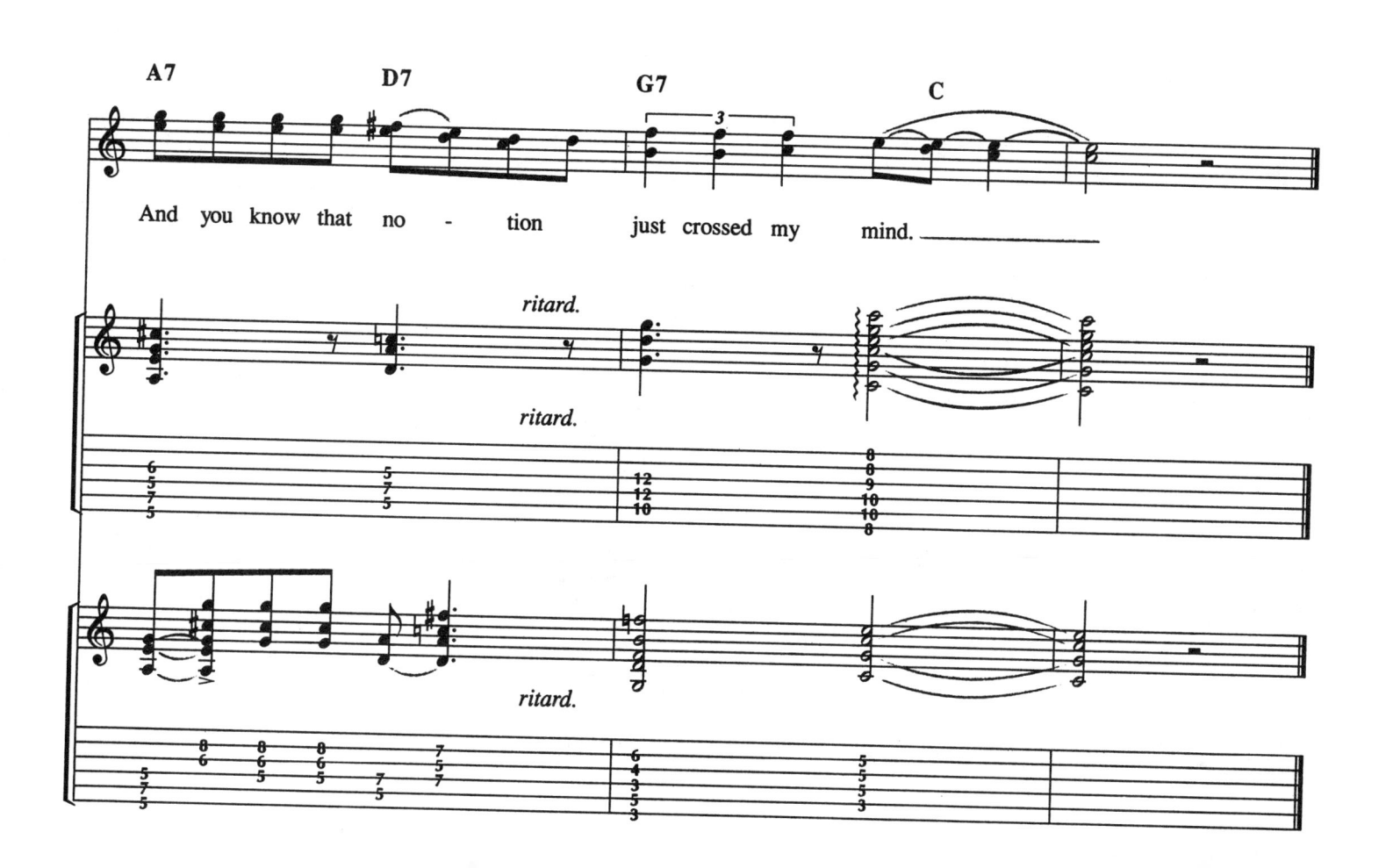

just crossed my mind.

And you know that no-tion just crossed my mind.

ritard.

CUMBERLAND BLUES

Words by
ROBERT HUNTER

Music by
JERRY GARCIA and PHILIP LESH

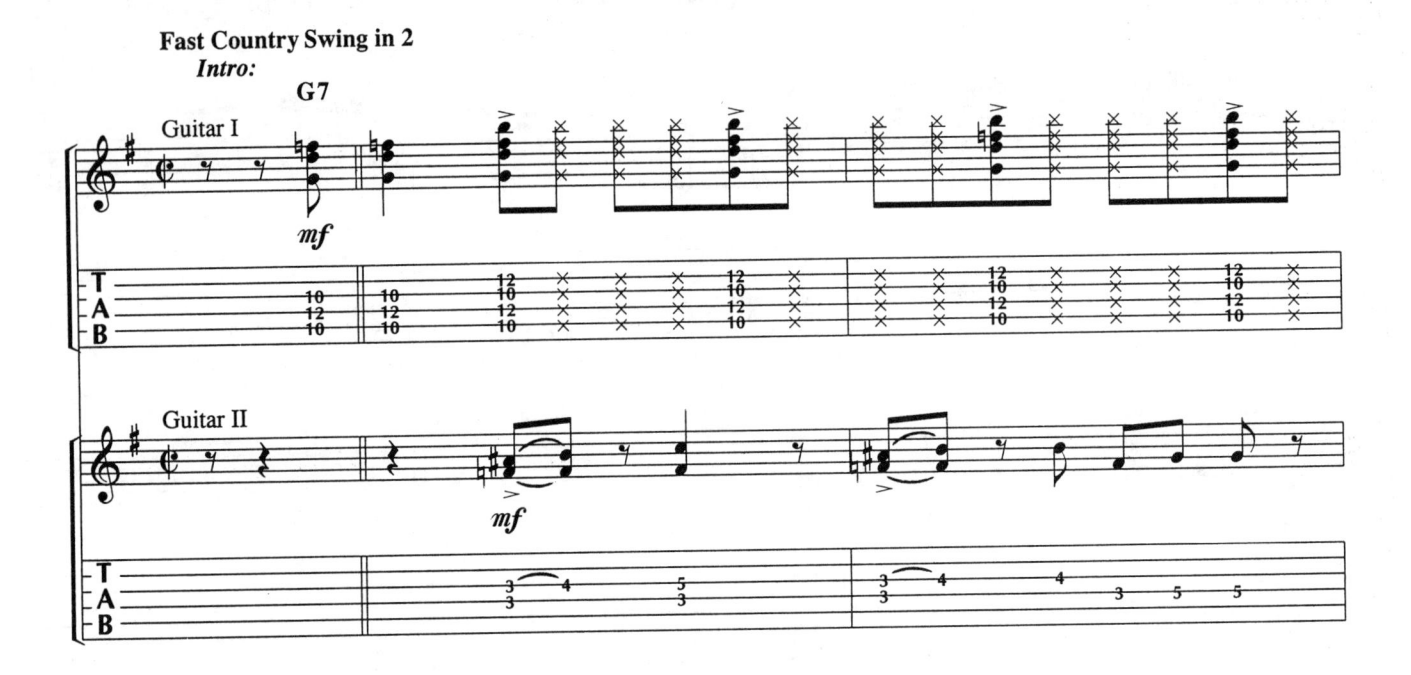

Fast Country Swing in 2
Intro:

61

I can't stay much long - er, Me - lin -

da; the sun is get - ting high.

I can't

help you ____ with your ____ trou - bles if

you won't help __ with __ mine. ____

I got-ta get down, I got-ta get down, got-ta get down to

Oo._____ to the mine.

67

keep me up just one more night;

I can't sleep here no

more. Lit-tle Ben

clock says quar-ter to eight, you

kept me up 'til four.

F#

I got-ta get down,

71

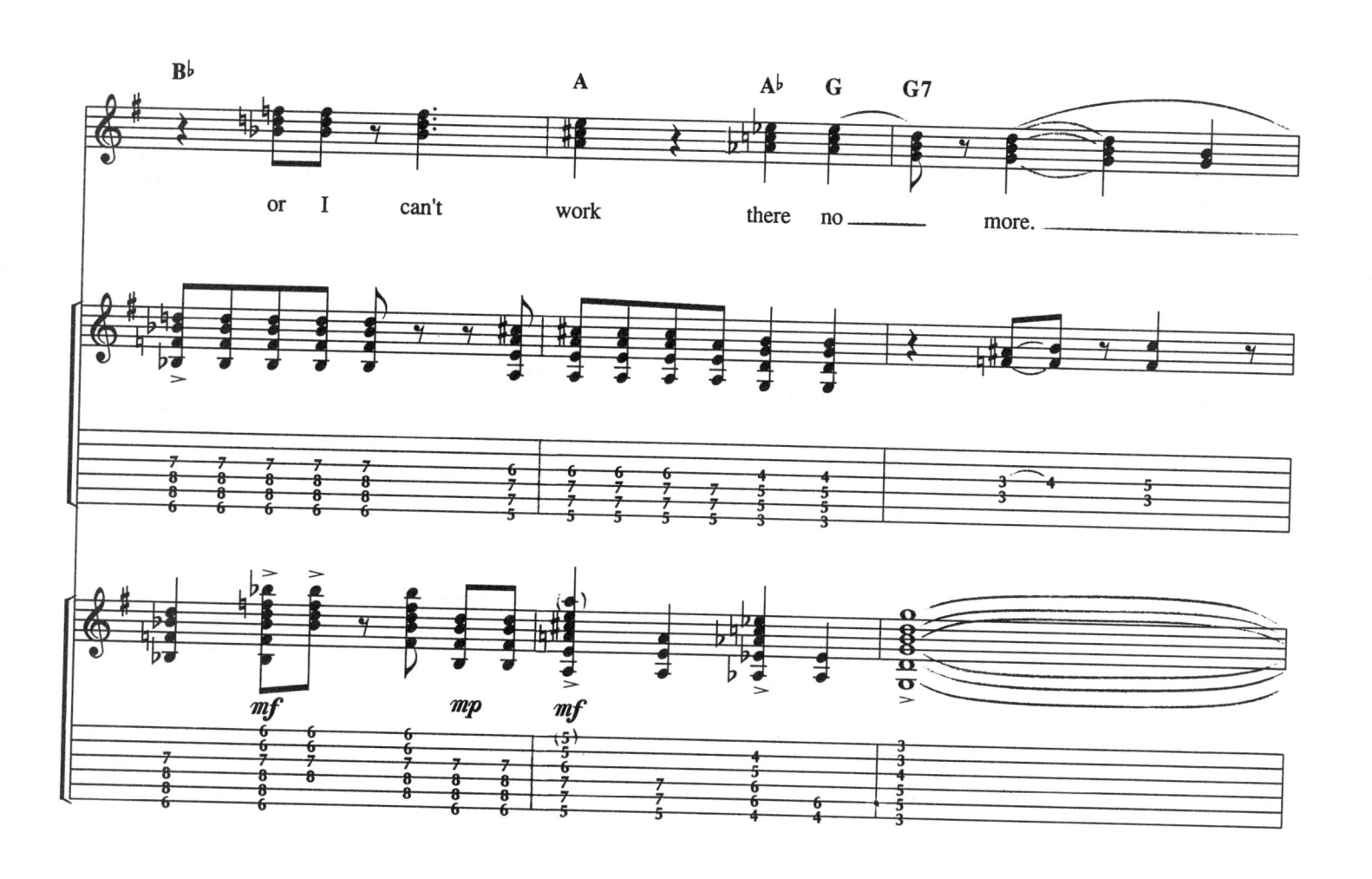

72

73

G
Gsus4
F♯7 G7
G
Gsus4
F♯7 G7
Rake
G
Gsus4
F♯7 G7
G
Gsus4
G7
f
mp
Guitar 4 (Acoustic)
mp
Let ring
mf

75

A lot-ta poor man make a five dol-lar bill,

will keep him hap-py all the time.

Some oth-er fel-lows mak-ing

Fade out

noth-ing at all and you can

Guitar 4

77

Enter Banjo

C

Can I go, Bud-dy, can I

D

go down, ___ take your shift at the mine? ___

C

Got-ta get down to the

Let ring

(got - ta get down to the Cum - ber - land mine)
Cum - ber - land mine; that's where I main - ly spend my time.

Make good mon - ey five dol - lars a day;

made an-y more___ I might___ move___ a - way.___

Lot-ta poor man got the Cum-ber-land blues; he can't win for los-ing. Lot-ta the poor man got to walk the line just to pay his un-ion dues.

I don't know now, I just don't know

if I'm going back again.

I don't know now, I just don't

(Fade in)

know _____ if I'm go-ing back __ a-gain. __

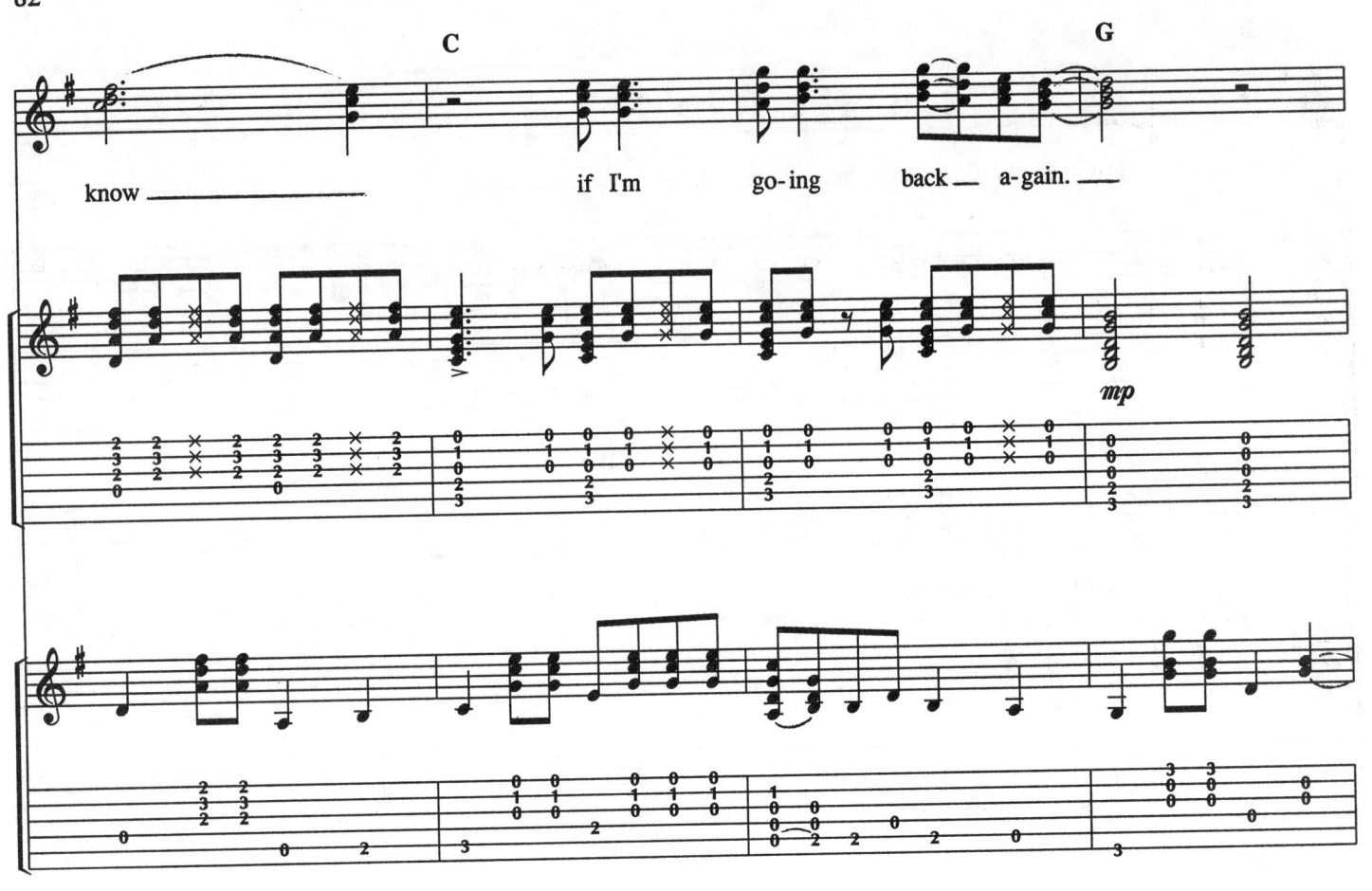

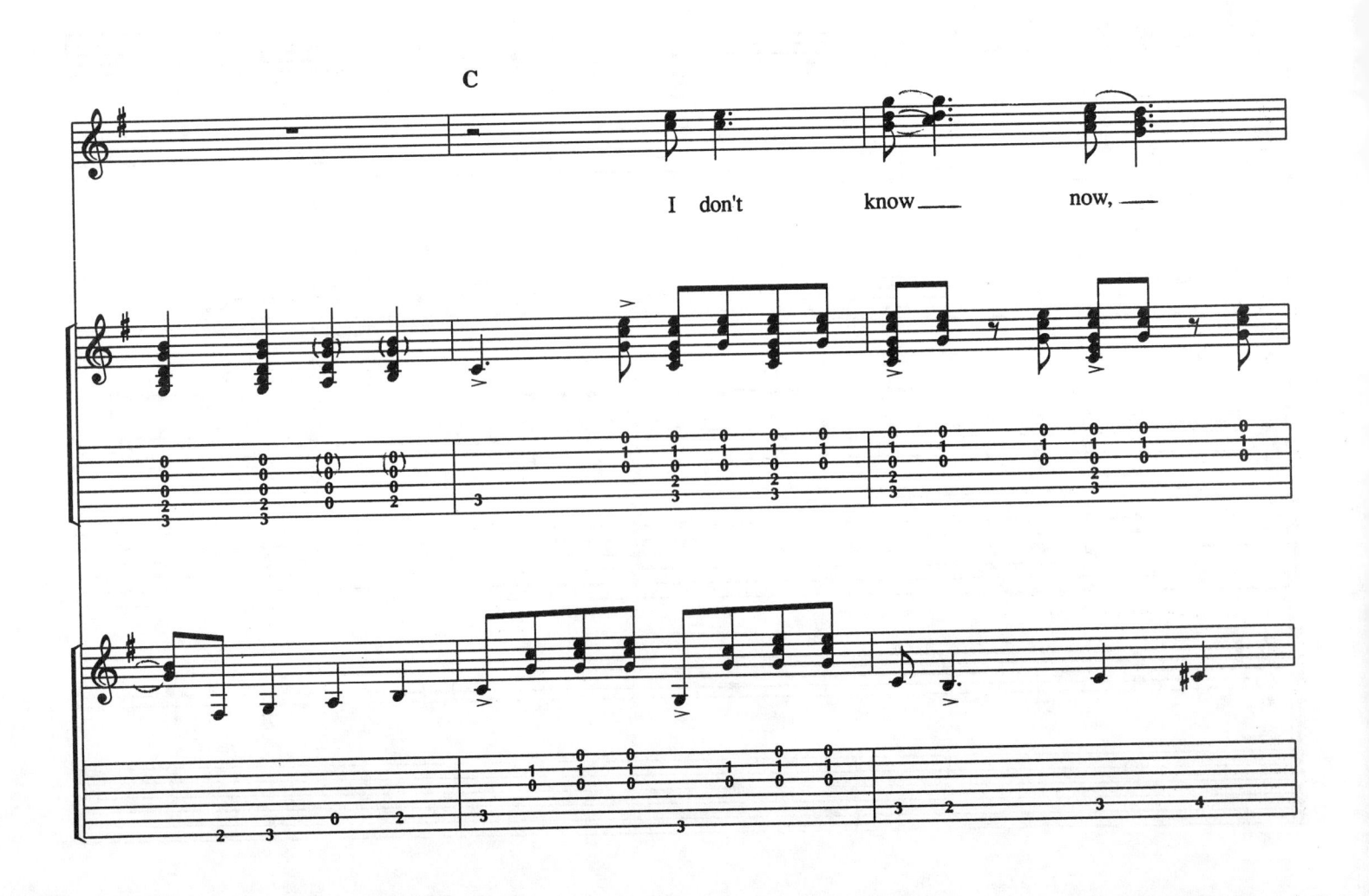

I don't know ___ now, __

I just don't know if I'm go-ing back a-gain.

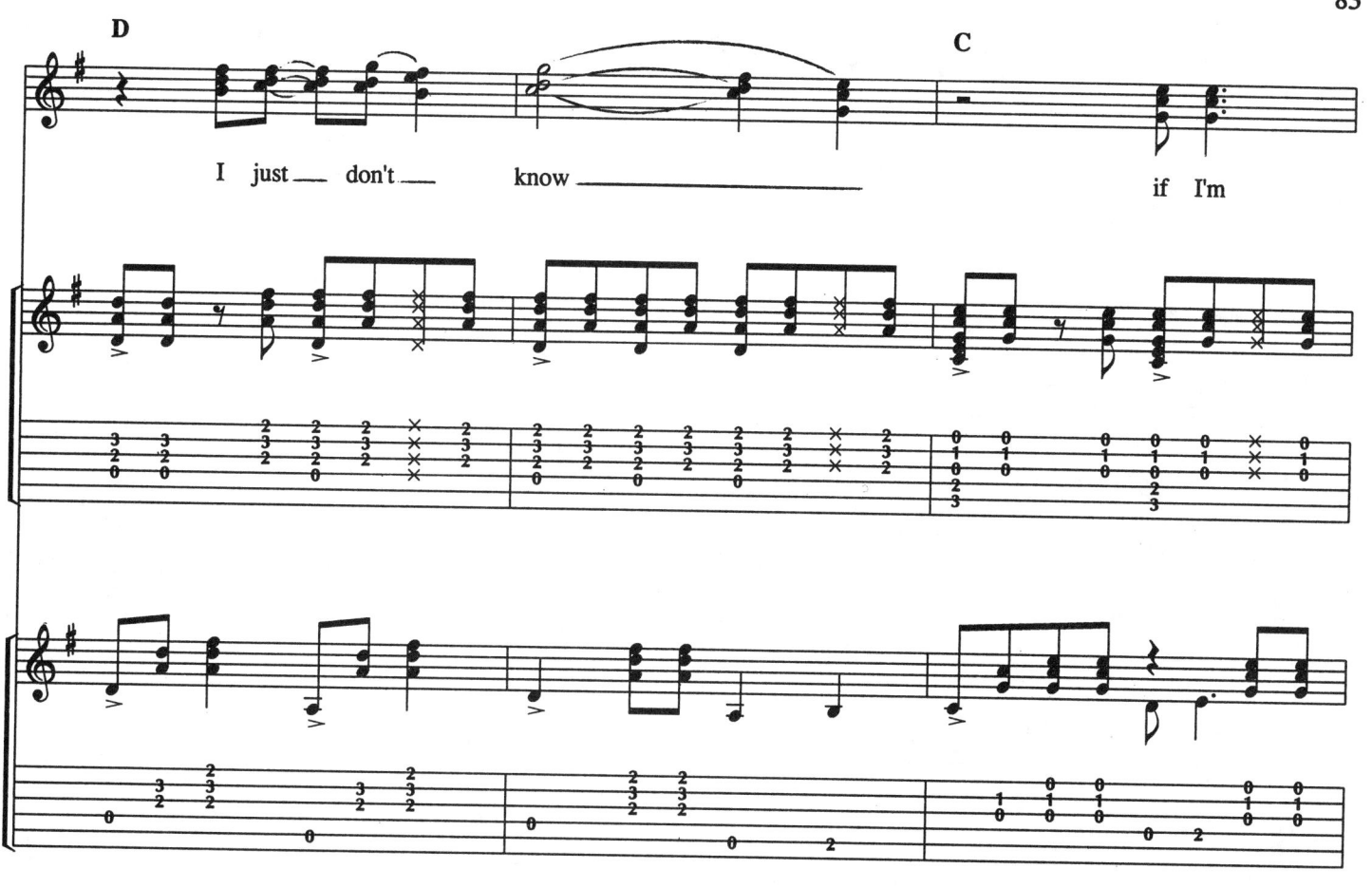

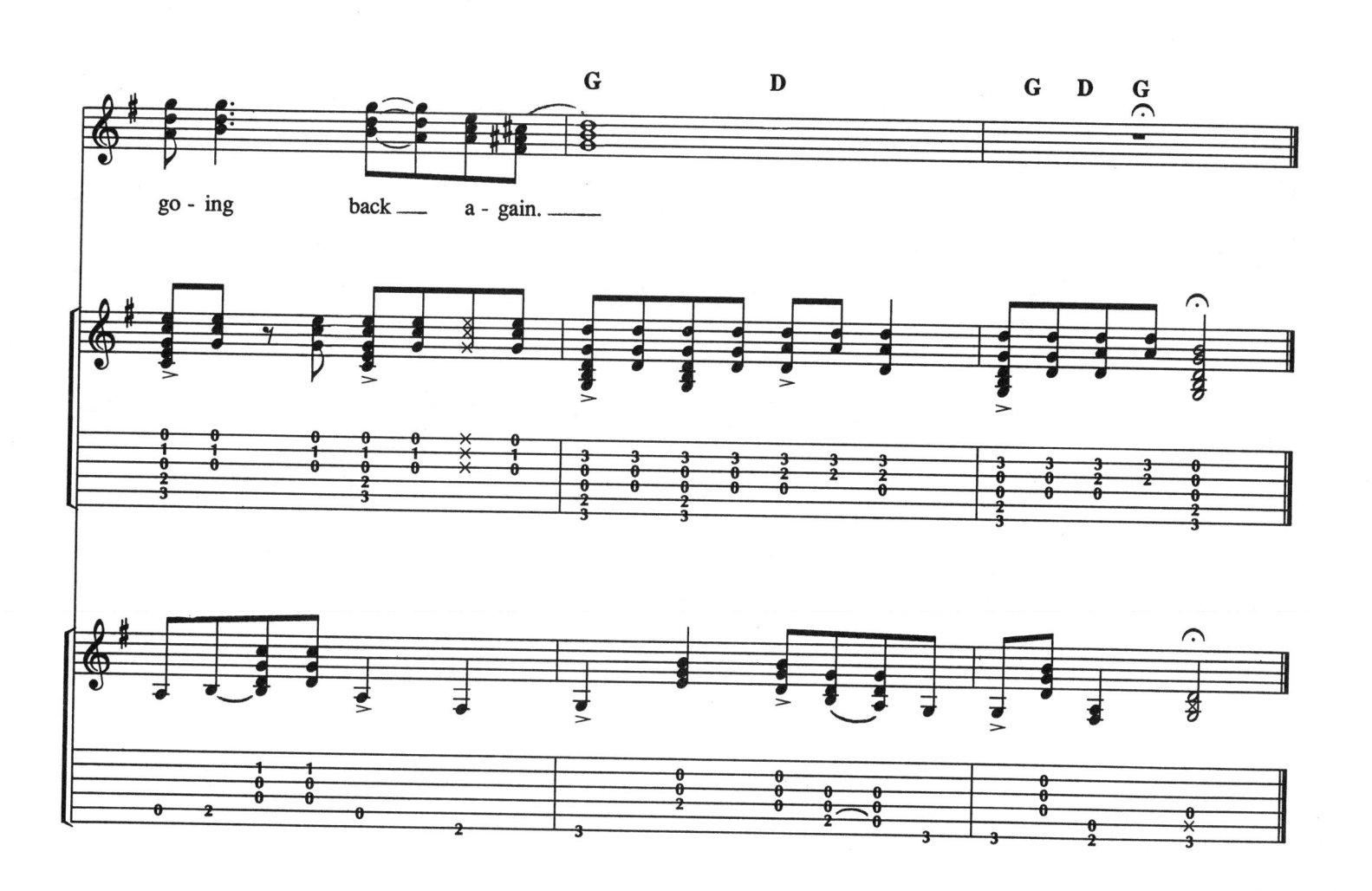

FRIEND OF THE DEVIL

Words by
ROBERT HUNTER

Music by
JERRY GARCIA and JOHN DAWSON

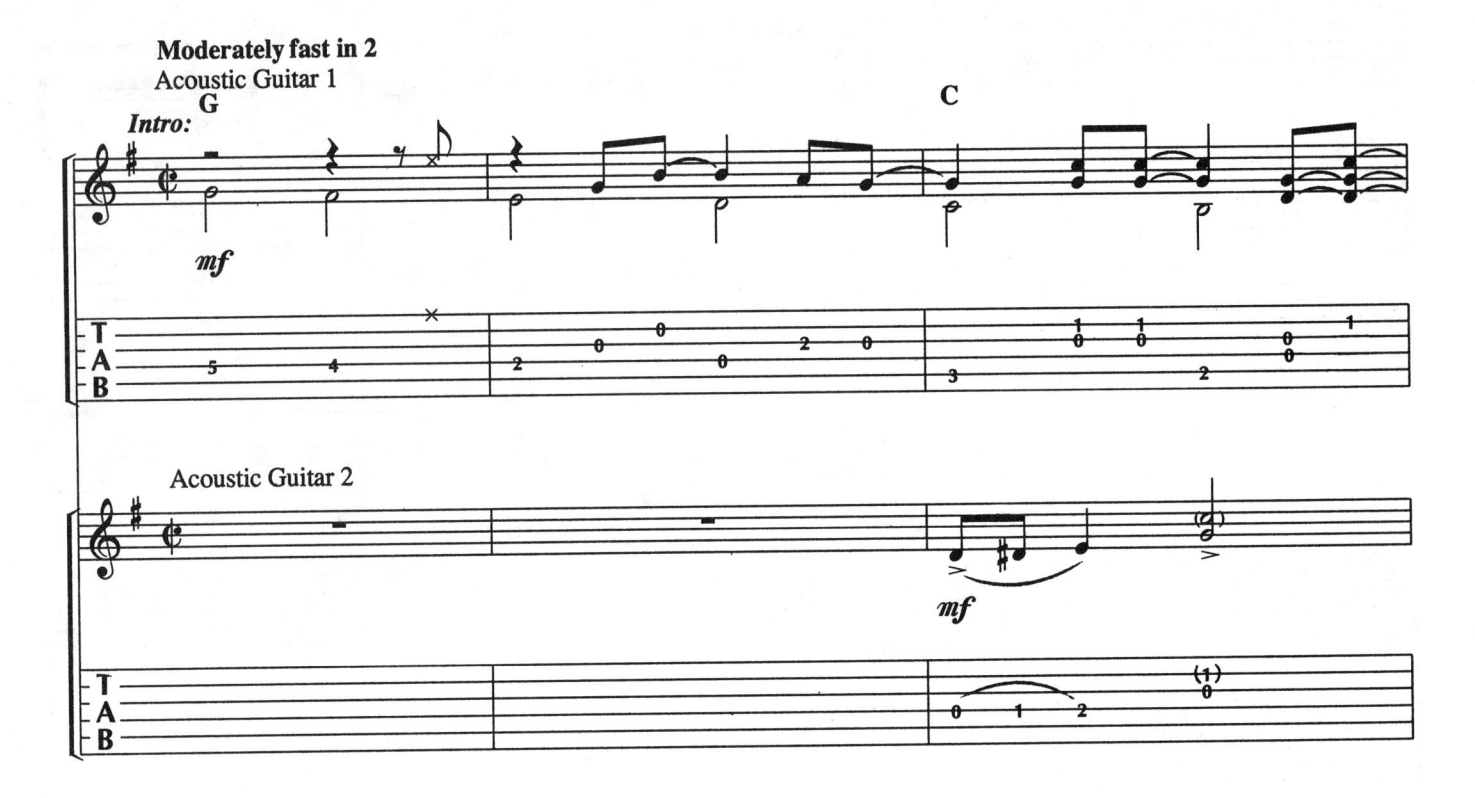

© 1970, 1991 ICE NINE PUBLISHING CO., INC.
All Rights Reserved

85

I lit out from Re-no, I was trailed by twen-ty hounds.

Did-n't get to sleep that night 'til the

morn-ing came a-round.___ Set out run-ning but I take my time,___ a friend of the de-vil is a friend of mine.___ If

88

I get home before daylight just might get some sleep tonight.

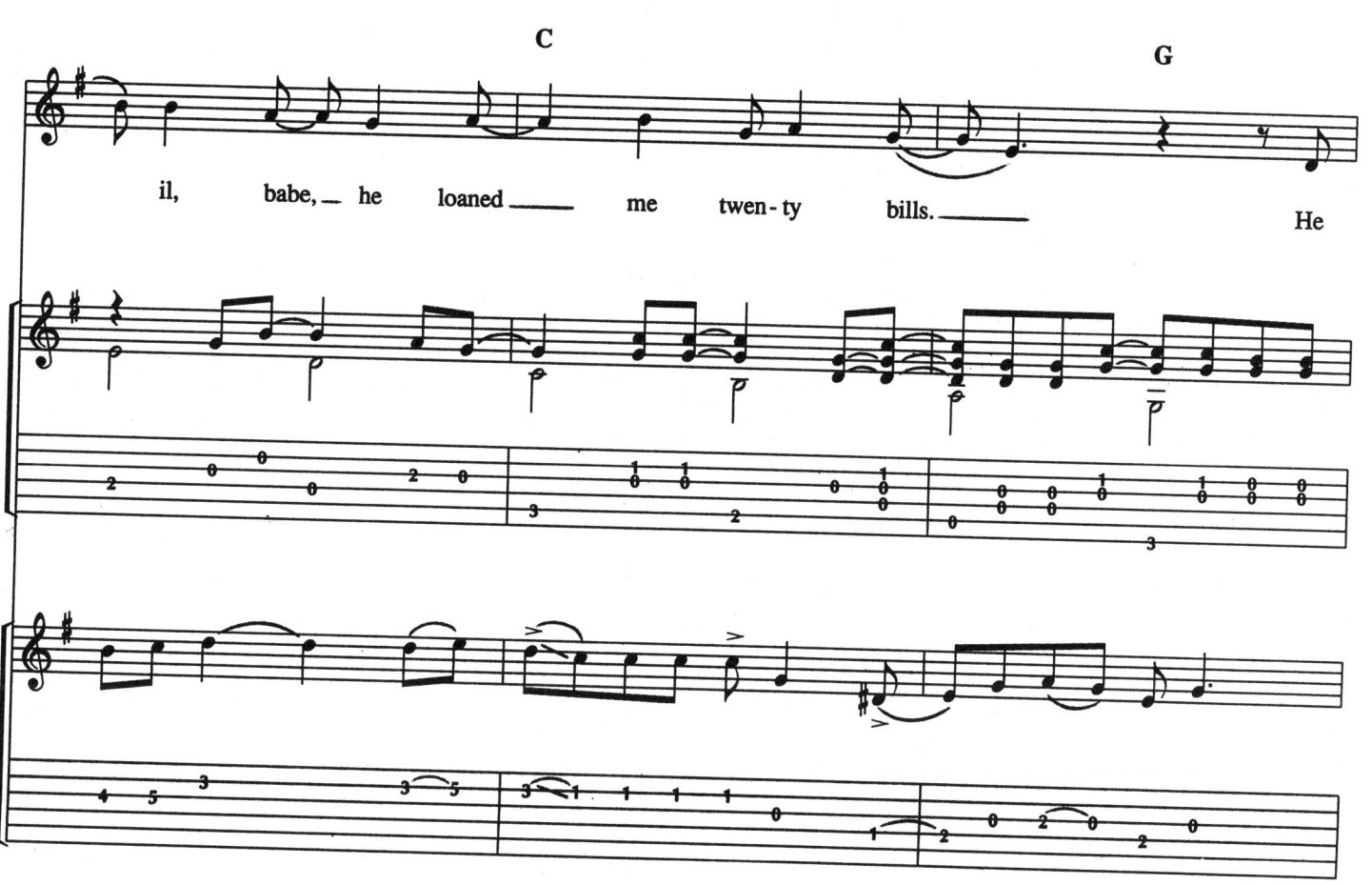

I ran into the dev-il, babe, he loaned me twenty bills. He

spent the night_ in U - tah in_ a cave_ up_ in the hills._

Set out run-ning but I take my time,_ a

Let ring

friend of the dev-il is a friend of mine. If I get home be-fore day-light just might get some sleep toni - ight.

ran down to the lev - ee but the dev - il caught me there.

He took my twen-ty dol-lar bill ___ and he
van - ished in the air. ___ Set out run-ning but I

Let ring

94

take my time, a friend of the dev-il is a friend of mine. If

I get home before day-light,

just might get some sleep to - ni - ight.

96

Bridge:

Got two reasons why I cry away each lonely night.

*The upstem notes are Mandolin, downstem notes are Guitar 2.

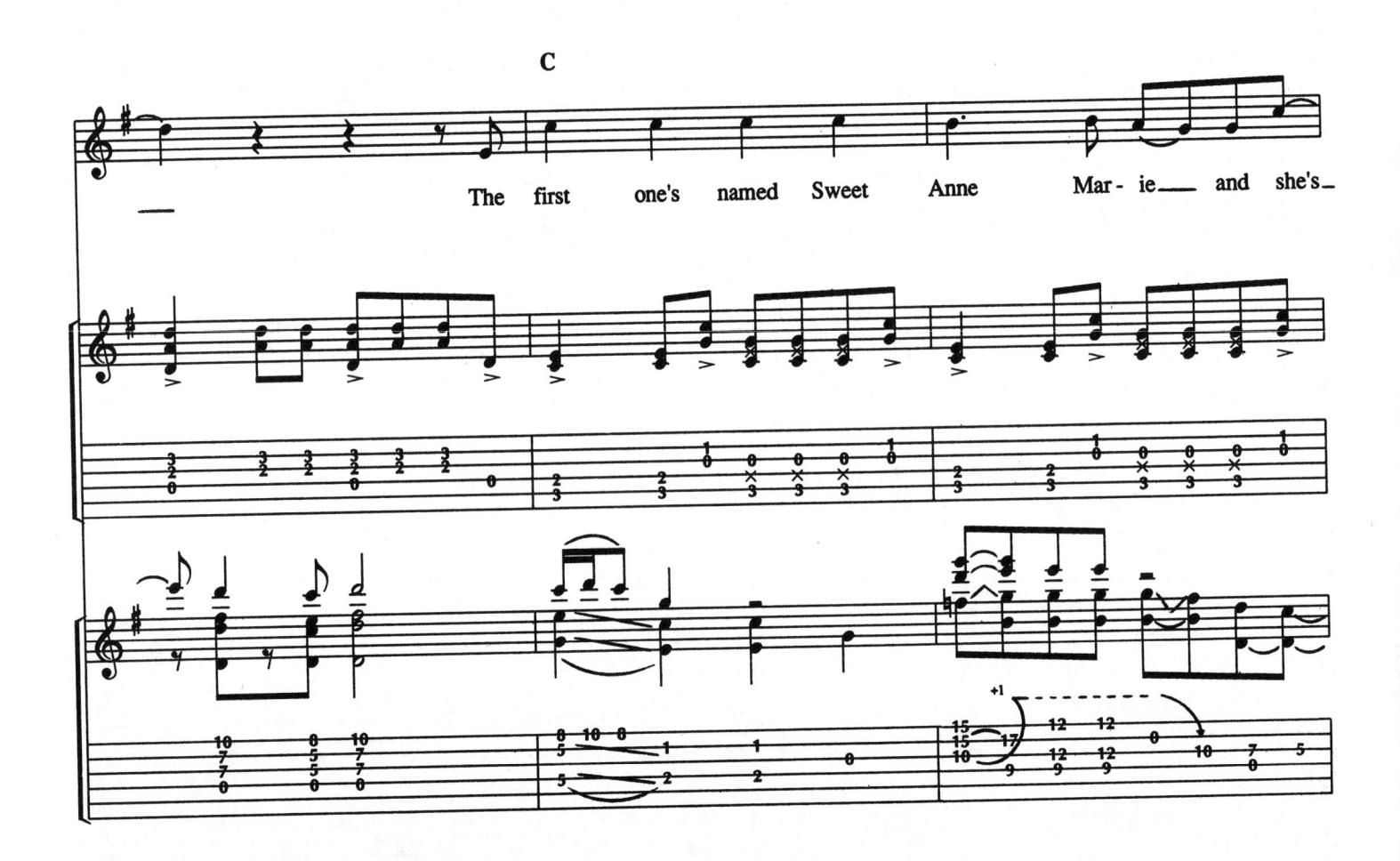

The first one's named Sweet Anne Marie and she's

my heart's de-light. Se-cond one is pris-on, ba-by, the sher-iff's on my trail and if he catch-es up with me ___ I'll spend my life in jail.

G
C
Got a wife in Chi-no, babe, and one in Cher - o - kee.
Let ring
G
First one says she's got my child, but

C
G
D
it don't look like me. Set out run-ning but I
Let ring
mf
mp
mf
D
Am
take my time, a friend of the dev - il is a friend of mine. If
mp
mf

I get home before daylight just might get some sleep tonight.

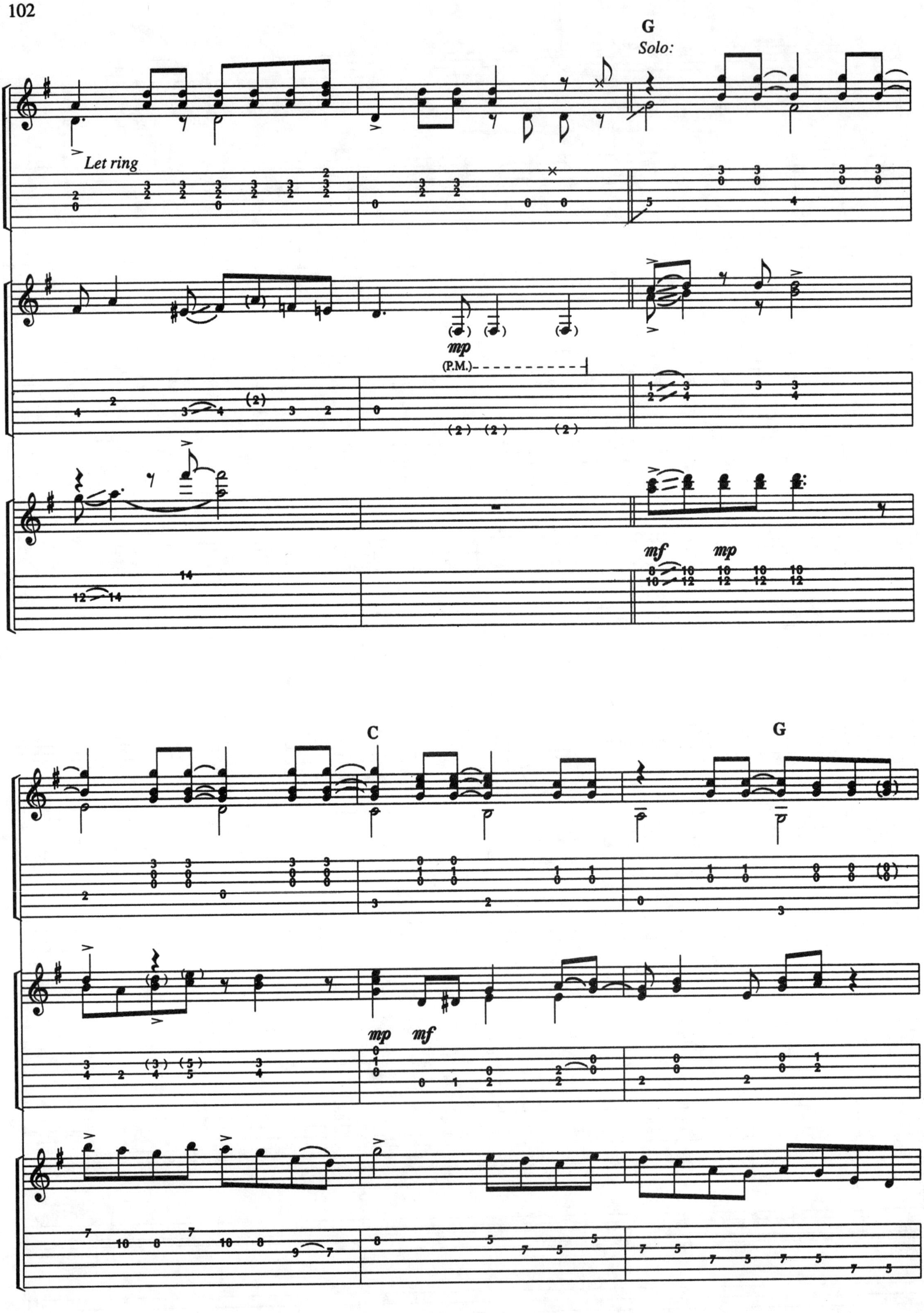
G
Solo:
Let ring
mp
(P.M.)
mf
mp
C
G
mp
mf

103

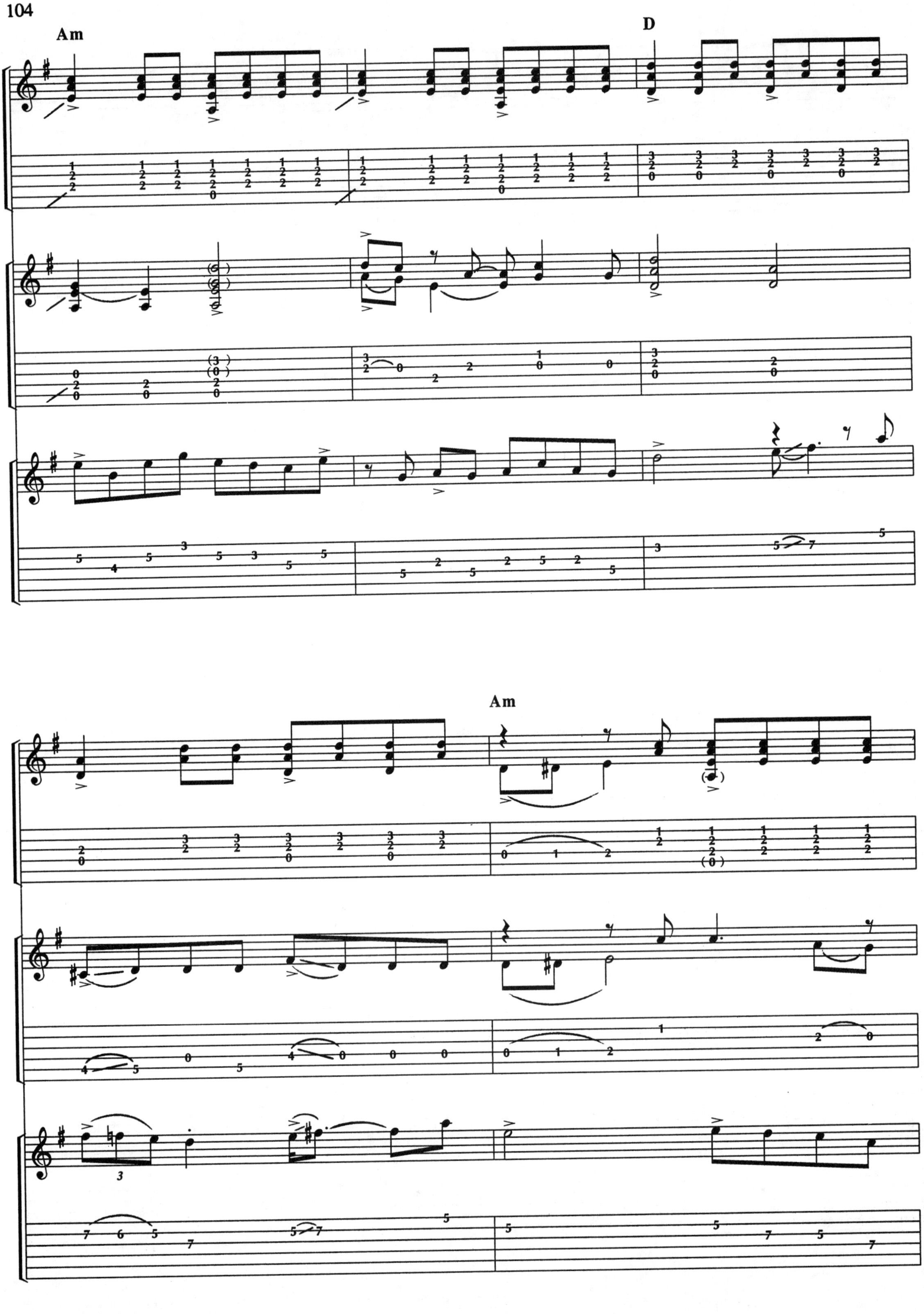
Am
D
Am

105

NEW SPEEDWAY BOOGIE

Words by
ROBERT HUNTER

Music by
JERRY GARCIA

Moderate Shuffle

Please — don't dom-i-nate the

© 1970, 1991 ICE NINE PUBLISHING CO., INC.
All Rights Reserved

rap, Jack, — if you got — nothing new — to say. — If — you — please, — don't back up — the track, — this — train — got — to run — to-day.

D♯7 E7
D♯7 E7
E°7
I spend a lit - tle time on the moun - tain,
E7
E5
A
E
E5
A
E7
E
E5
E7
E
spent a lit - tle time on the hill. (on the hill) I heard some say "Bet - ter
mp
+1/4

109

run a-way," others say "Bet-ter stand still." Now

I don't know but I've been told it's hard to run with the

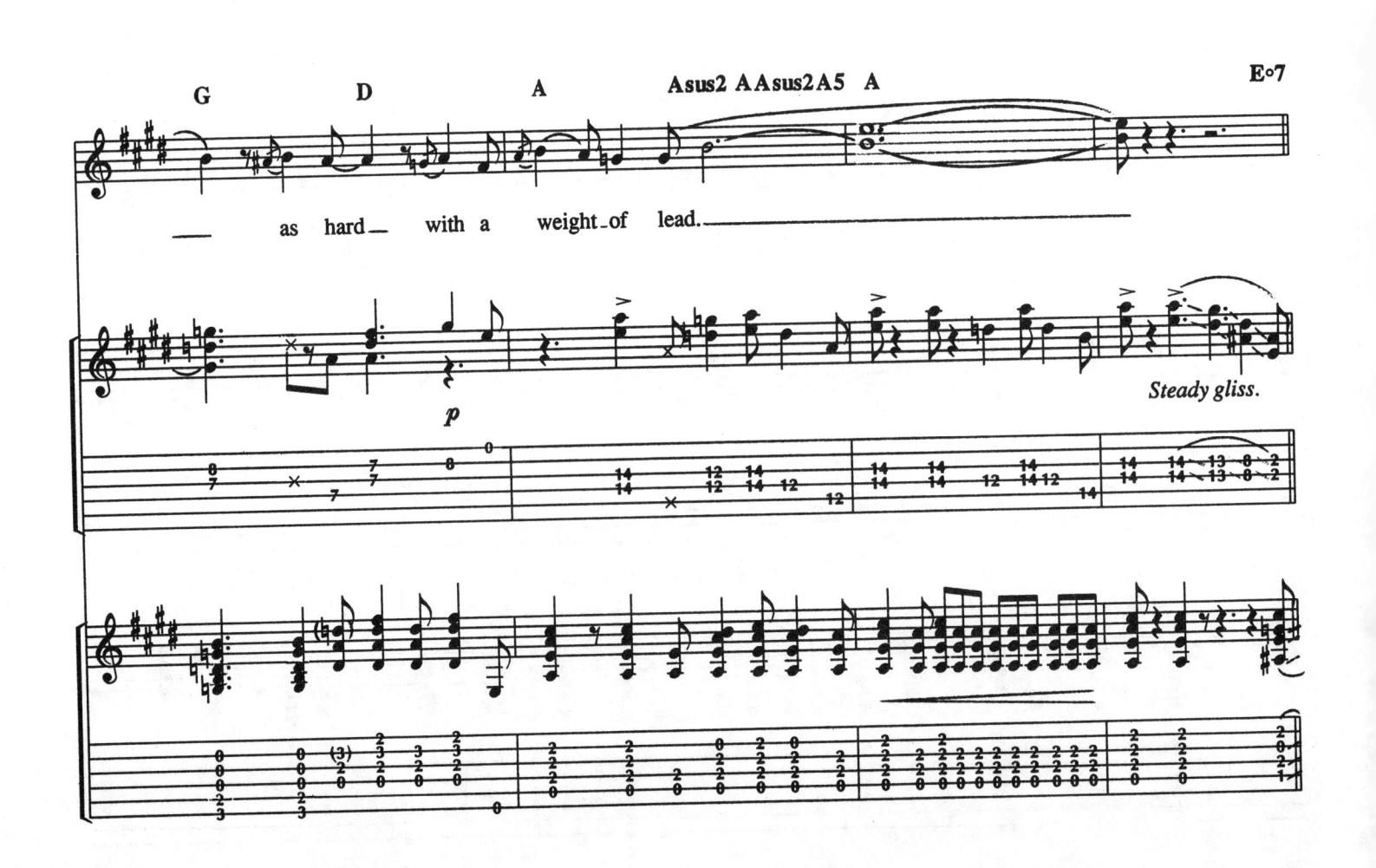

weight of gold. The oth-er hand I had heard it said, it's just as hard with a weight of lead.

Who— can de - ny,— who can de - ny— it's— not—

112

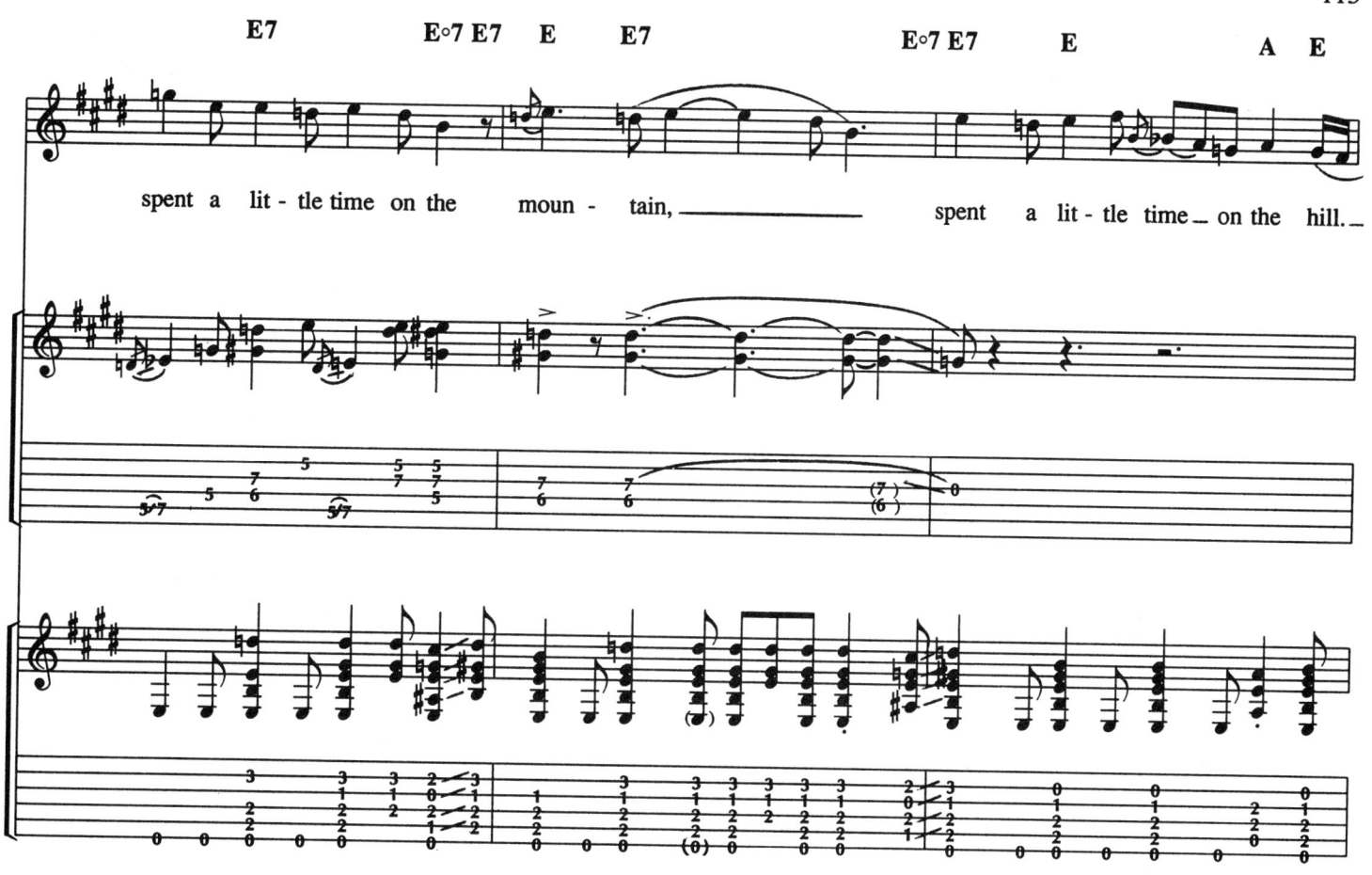

spent a lit-tle time on the moun-tain, _____ spent a lit-tle time_ on the hill._

_ (on the hill)_____ Things__ went down_ we don't_ un-der-stand_ but I think_

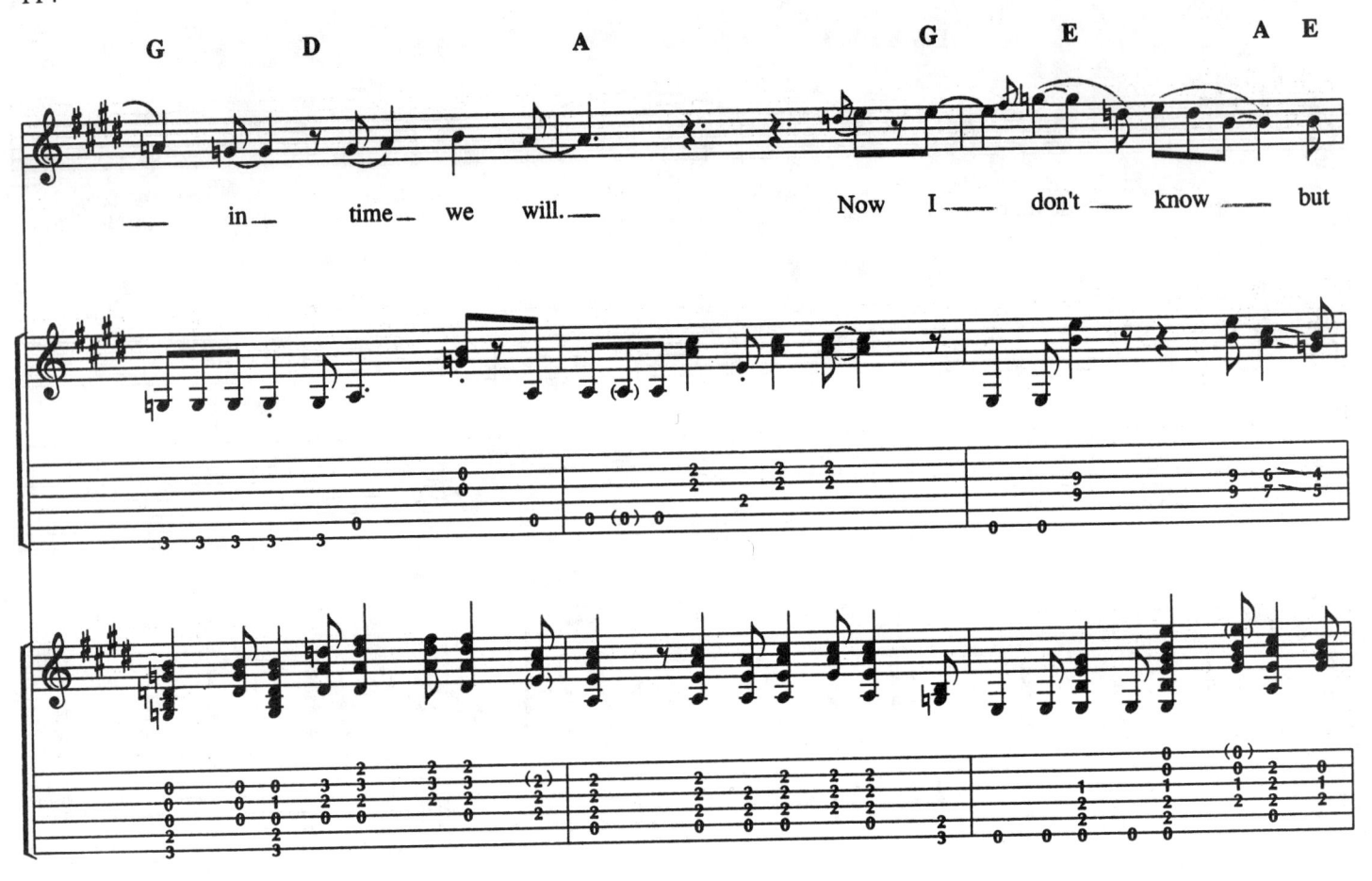

in time we will. Now I don't know but I was told in the heat of the sun a man died of cold.

Keep on ____ com-ing or ____ stand ____ and wait, ____ with the sun ____ so dark and the

(Hour so late) ____
hour ____ so late. ____

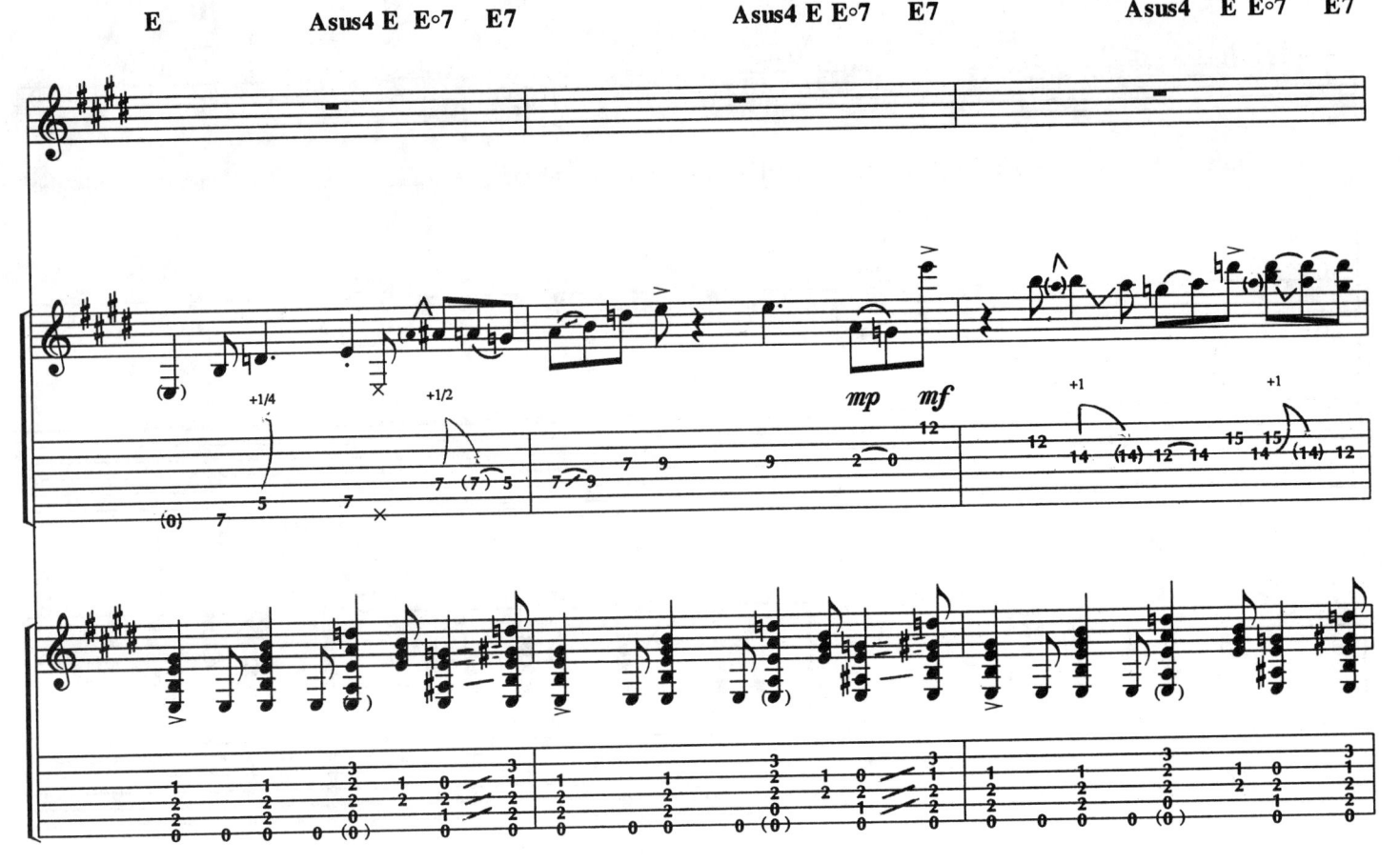

You can't over look the lack, Jack, of an-

y other highway to ride. It's got no signs or dividing lines, and very few rules to guide. I spent a lit-tle time on the moun-tain, _____ spent a lit-tle time on the hill.

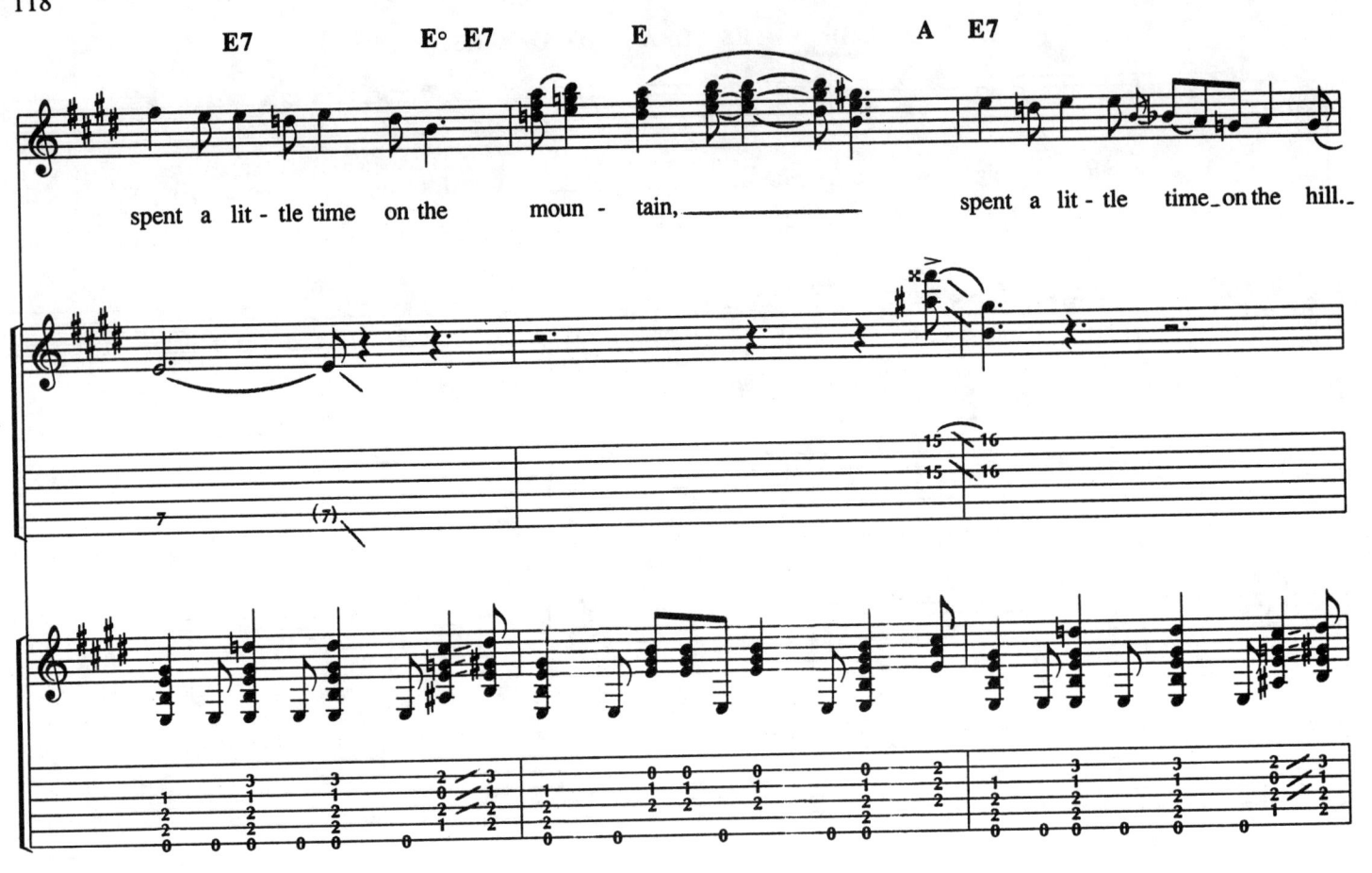

— (on the hill.) _____ Well, I saw things getting out of hand, _____ I guess

119

I don't know who's back's that strong; may-be find out be-fore too long.

121

122

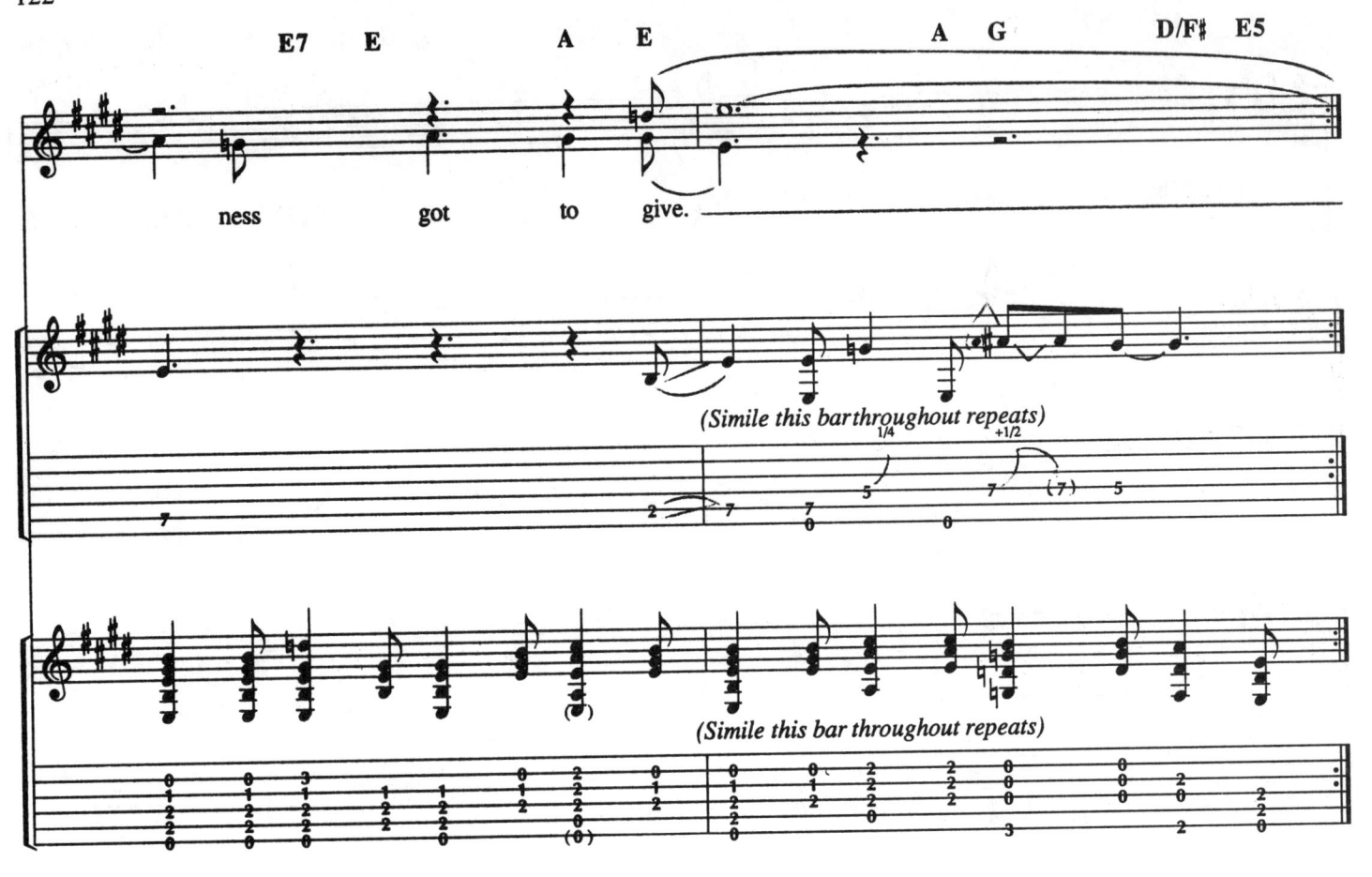

ness got to give.

123

RIPPLE

Words by ROBERT HUNTER

Music by JERRY GARCIA

© 1971, 1991 ICE NINE PUBLISHING CO., INC.
All Rights Reserved

125

If my words did glow with the gold of sunshine

if your cup be empty,

(Let ring throughout)

Mandolin *(on D.S. only)*

and my tunes ___ were played ___ on ___ the harp ___
if your cup ___ is full, ___ may ___ it be ___

On D.S. only

__ un - strung, ___ would you hear my voice ___
__ a - gain. ___ Let it ___ be known ___

come through the music? Would you hold
there is a foun - tain

it near, as it were your own?
that was not made by the hands of men.

— It's a hand me down, the thoughts are
— There is a road, no sim-ple

— bro - ken perhaps they're
— high - way be- tween the

better left unsung. I don't know;
dawn and the dark of night. And if you go,

don't really care.
no one may follow;

Let there be songs to fill the air.
that path is for your steps a-lone.

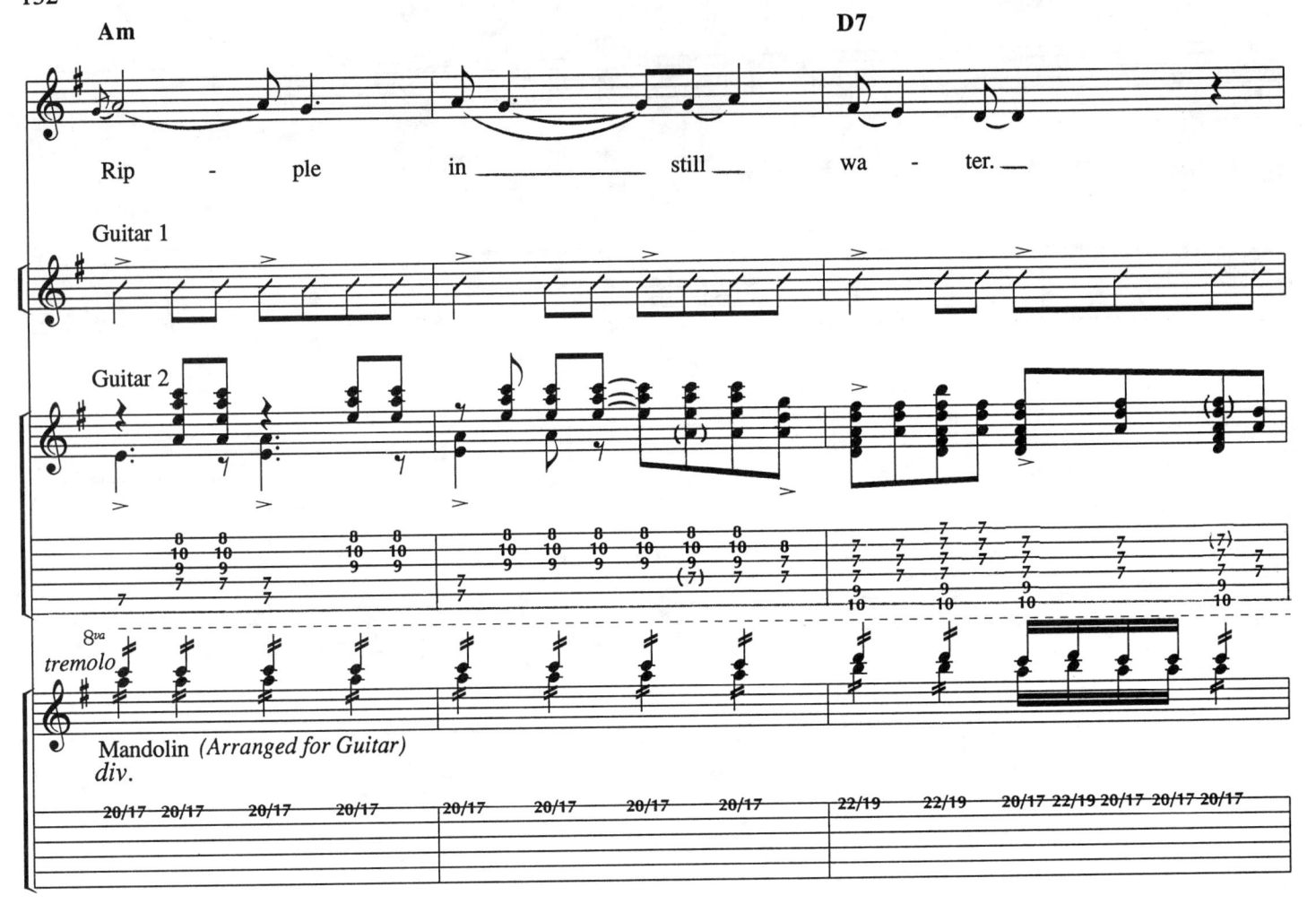

Rip - ple in _____ still __ wa - ter. _____ when there is __ no __ peb - ble tossed, __ nor

133

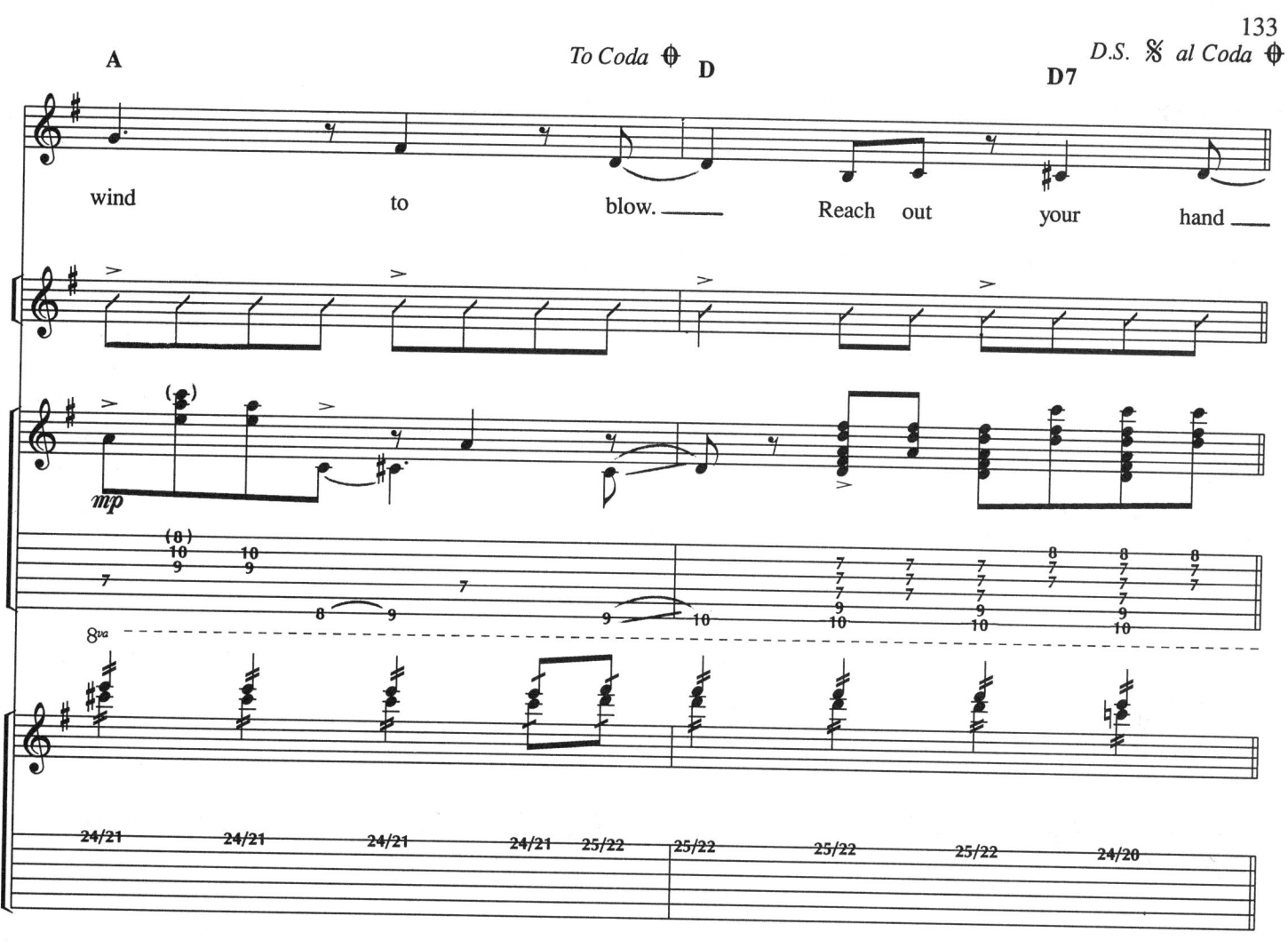

*The upstem notes are Mandolin, downstem notes are Guitar 2

fol-low, but if you fall, you fall a-lone. If you should stand then who's to guide you.

Lyrics:

If I knew the way I would take you home. La dee da, da, da la da da da da,

Mandolin

136

137

SUGAR MAGNOLIA

Words by
ROBERT HUNTER and BOB WEIR

Music by
BOB WEIR

*Pedal Steel (Arranged for Guitar)
(1st bar only)

© 1970, 1991 ICE NINE PUBLISHING CO., INC.
All Rights Reserved

139

Verse 1:

Sug-ar Mag-no-lia, blos-soms bloom-ing, heads all emp-ty and I____ don't care.____ Saw my ba-by down_

Guitars 1 & 2

by the river, _____ *knew she'd have to come up soon for air.* _____

Verse 2:
Sweet blos - som, come on un - der the wil - low, _____ we can have high _____ times if you'll a - bide. We can dis - cov - er the won - ders of na - ture, _____ roll - ing in the rush - es down _____

141

pays my tick-et when I speed.
laz-ing in the sun light, yes, in deed.

Verse 3:

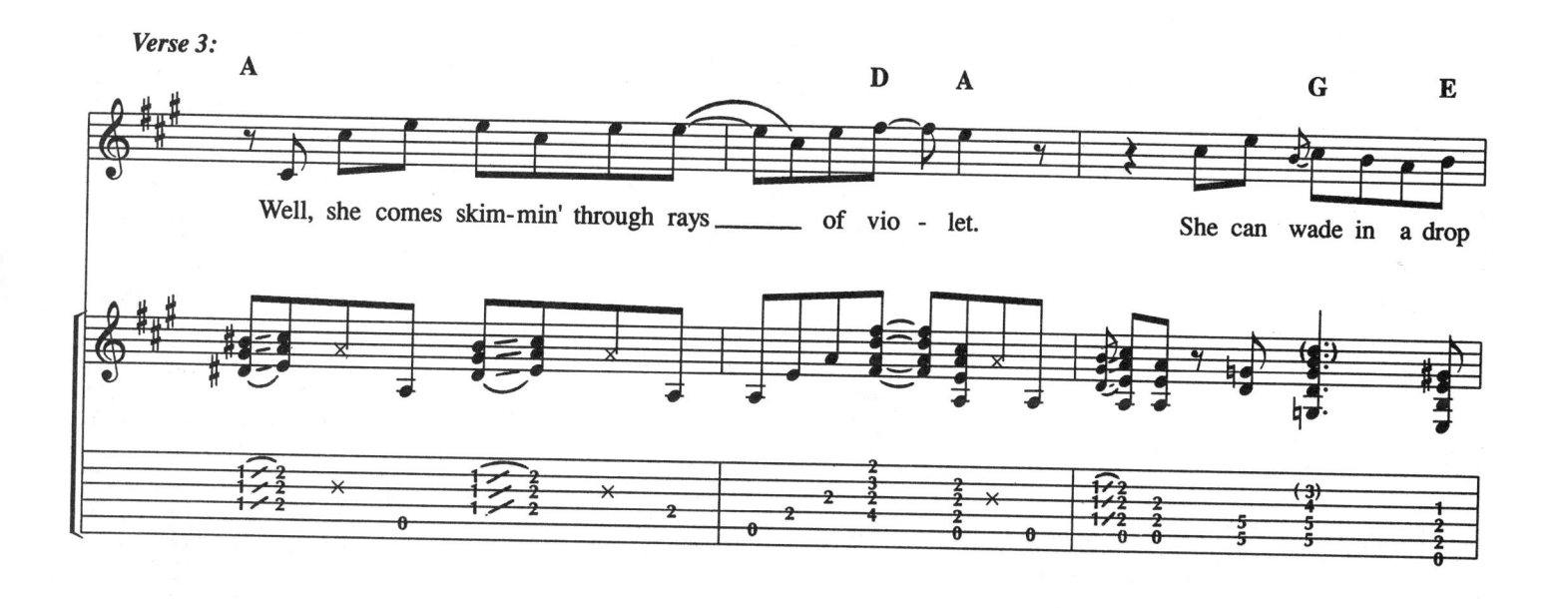

Well, she comes skim-min' through rays _____ of vio - let. She can wade in a drop of dew. ____ she don't come and I don't ___ fol - low, waits back stage while I sing to you.

Verse 4:
Well, she can dance a Cajun rhythm, jump like a willys in four wheel drive. She's a summer love in the spring, fall and winter; she can make happy any man alive.

145

146

147

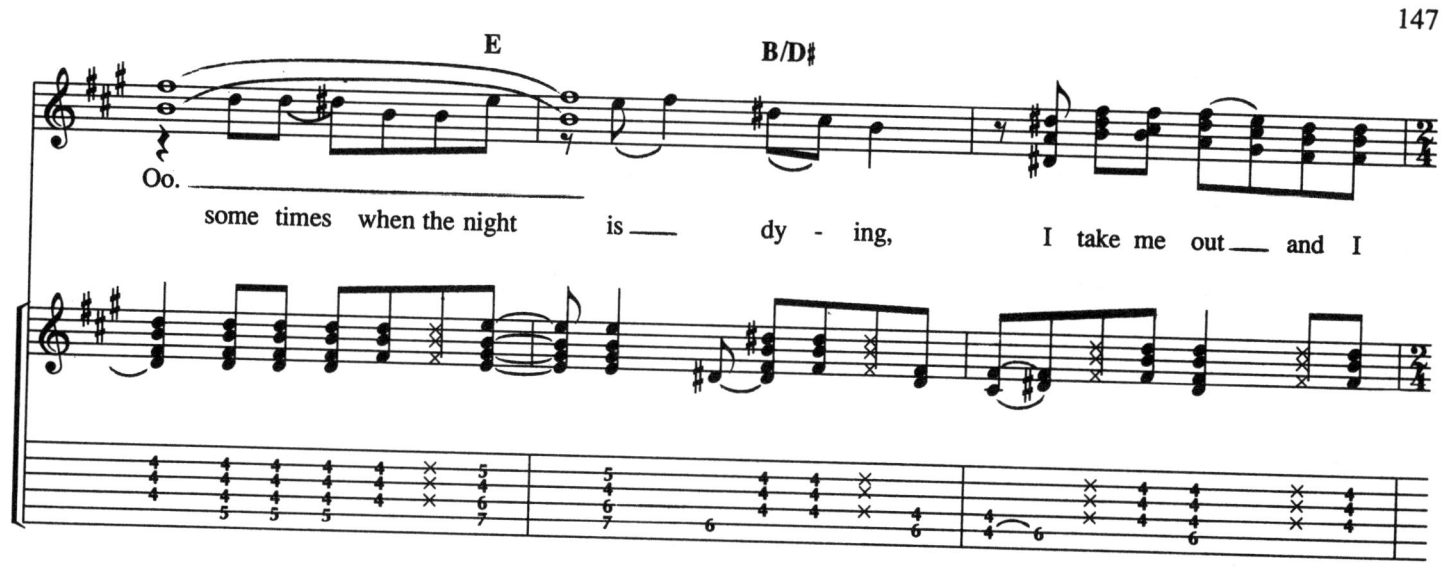

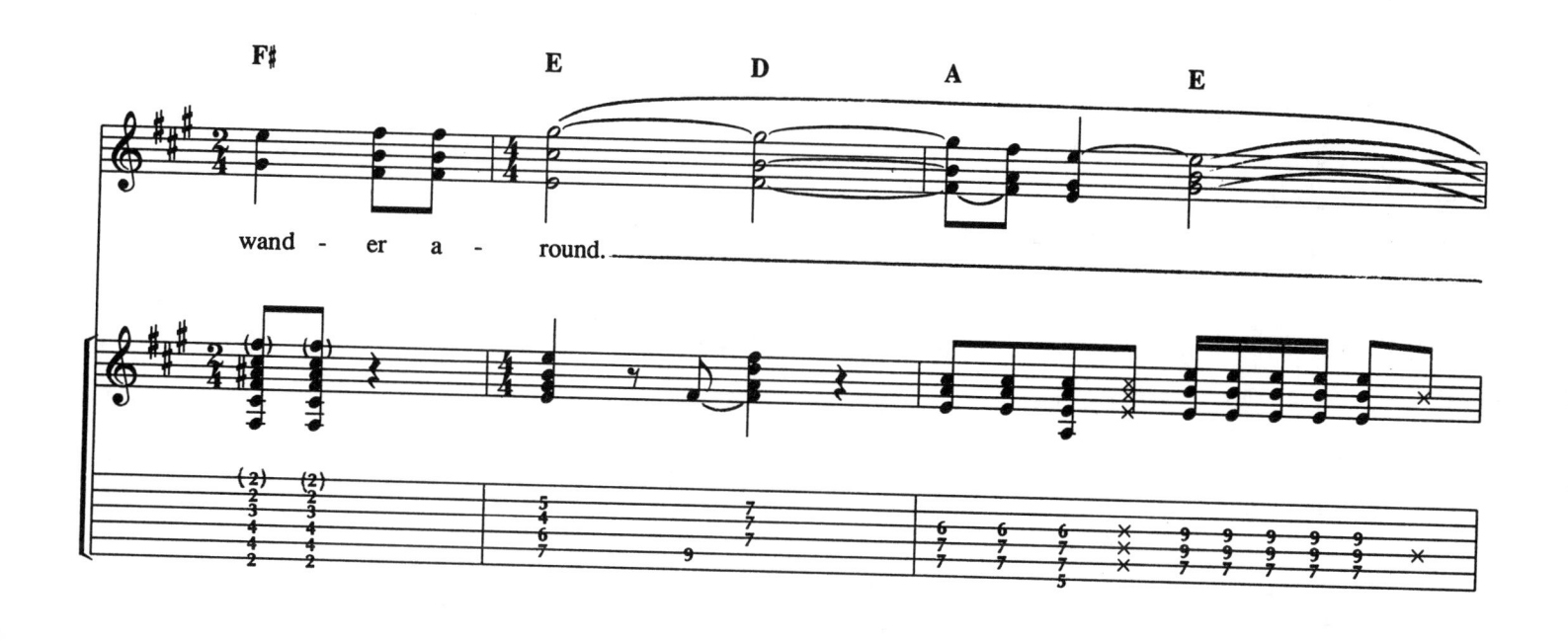

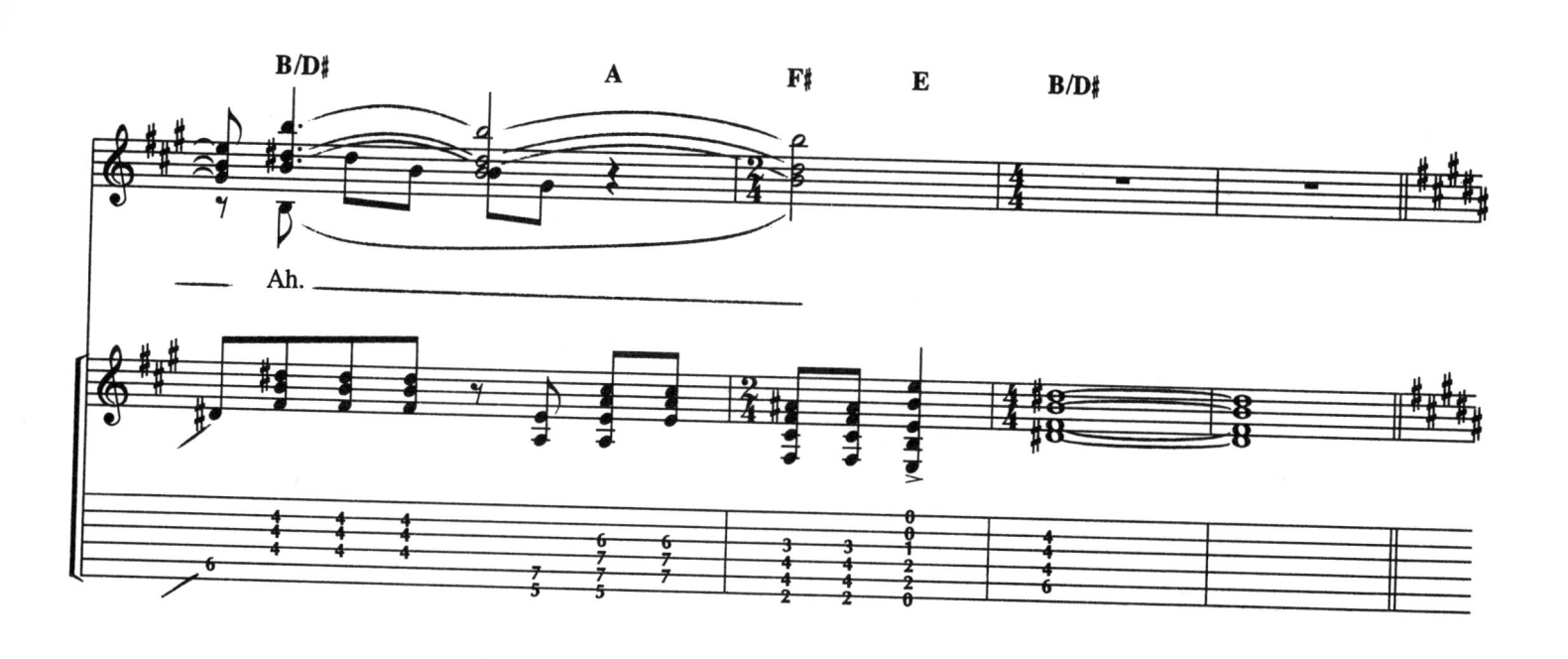

Oo. _____ some times when the night is ____ dy - ing, I take me out ____ and I wand - er a - round. _____ Ah. _____

B E B E B F♯
The sun - shine day - dream,
(Background Vocals)
Doo doo doo doo doo doo doo doo, doo doo doo doo doo
E B E B E
walk-ing in the tall trees. Go - in' where the wind goes.
doo doo doo. Doo doo doo doo doo doo doo doo.
B F♯ E B E B E
Bloom-in' like a red rose. Breath-in' more
Doo doo doo doo doo doo doo doo. Doo doo doo doo doo doo doo doo.

freely.___ Ride out sing-in', I'll walk you in the mornin' sun-shine.___

Doo doo doo doo doo doo doo doo. Doo doo doo doo doo doo doo doo,

The sun-shine_ day_ dream.___ Sun-

doo doo doo doo doo doo doo doo. Doo doo doo doo

shine_ day_ dream.___ A walk-in' in the sun-shine

doo doo_ doo doo, doo doo doo doo doo doo doo doo.

TRUCKIN'

Words by ROBERT HUNTER

Music by JERRY GARCIA, BOB WEIR and PHIL LESH

© 1971, 1991 ICE NINE PUBLISHING CO., INC.
All Rights Reserved

151

Oo, _____ yeah. _____

Chorus:

Truck-in', ___ got ___ my chips cashed in, ___ keep ___ truck-in', ___ like the

Guitar 1

Guitar 3

A
B
A A♯ B
doo - dah man.. To - geth - er, more or less in line.
A
8va
loco
8va
+1
21
+1
19 19
A
E
Just keep truck - in' on.
8va
17
Guitar 3 tacet

153

Guitar 2

(Fade in)

Verse 1:

E5 E6 E5   E5 E6 E5   E6 E5   E6 E5   E6   E5   E7 E6 E5

Ar-rows of ne-on and flash-ing mar-quees out on Main Street, — Chi - ca-go, New York, De-troit and it's all on the

154

same street. Your typ-i-cal cit-y in-volved in a typ-i-cal day dream,

hang it up and see what to-mor-row brings.

Chorus:

Dal - las got a soft ma - chine. Hous - ton, too close to New Or - leans. New York got the ways an' means but

156

just won't let _ you be. _____

(Enter Keys)

Verse 2:
E E5 E6 E5 E7 E5 E6 E5 E6 E5
Most of the cats that you meet on the street speak of true love,
Guitar 1
E6 E5 E7 E5 E6 E5 E6 E5 E7 E5
most of the time they're sit - tin' and cry - in at home.
E6 E5 E6 E5 E6 E5 E7 E5
One of these days, they know they got - ta get go - in'
E6 E5 E6 E7 E5 E6 E5
out of that door and down to the street all a - lone.

Chorus:

Truck-in', ___ like the doo-dah ___ man, ___ once told ___ me you got to play your ___ hand. ___ Some-times, ___ the cards ain't worth a dime ___

if you don't lay 'em down.

160

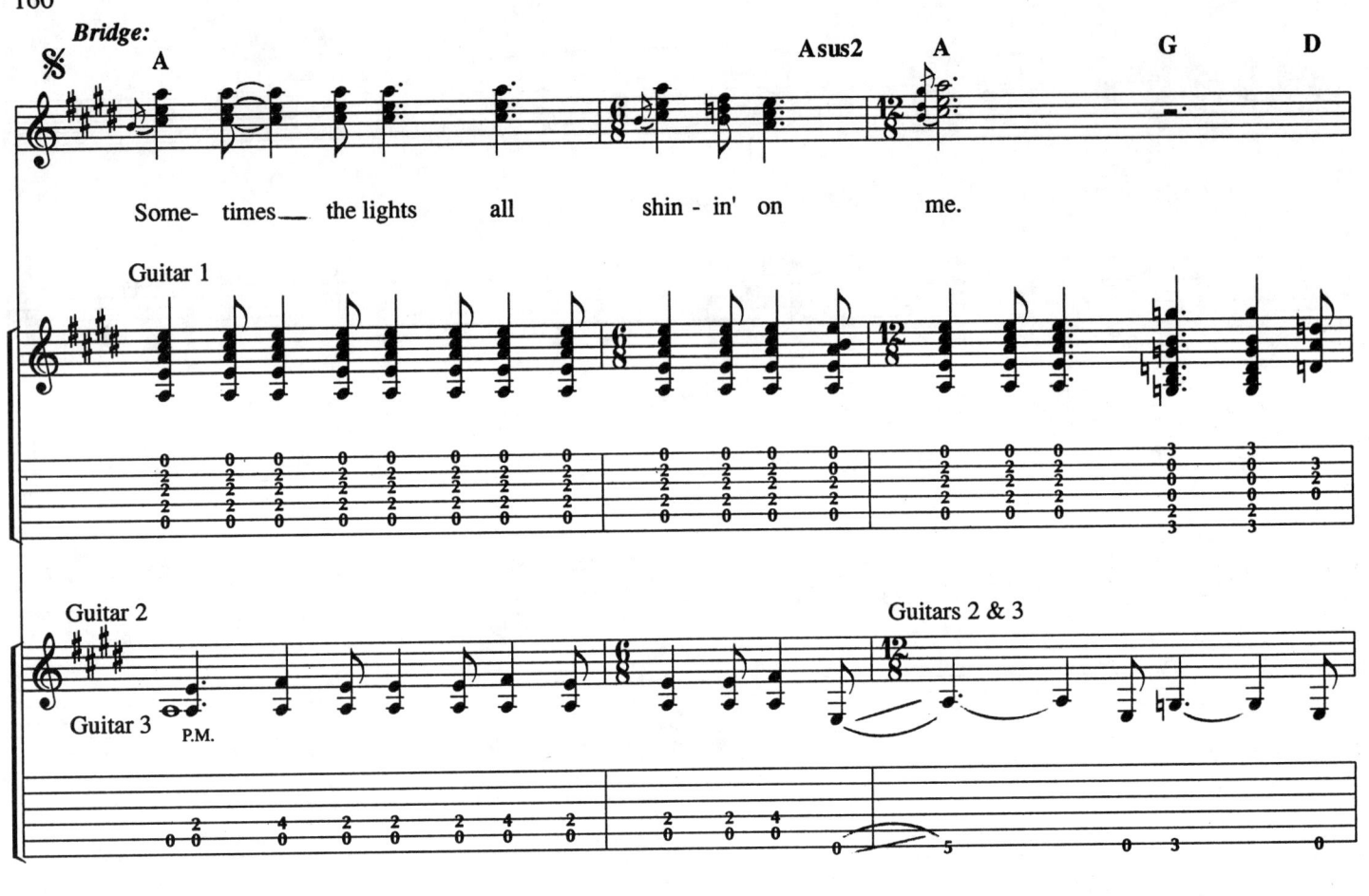

see. Lately it oc- curs to me what a

long, _____ strange trip it's _____ been. _____

Verse 3:
E5 E6 E7 E6 E5 E6 E5 E6 E5 E6 E5 E6 E5 E6 E5
What in the world ev- er be came_ of Sweet Jane?_ She lost her spark le, you know she is- n't the
Guitar 1
Guitar 3
E6 E5 E6 E5 E6 E5 E6 E5 E6 E5 E6 E5
same._ Liv-in' on reds, vit- a- min C_ and co- caine, ______
loco

164

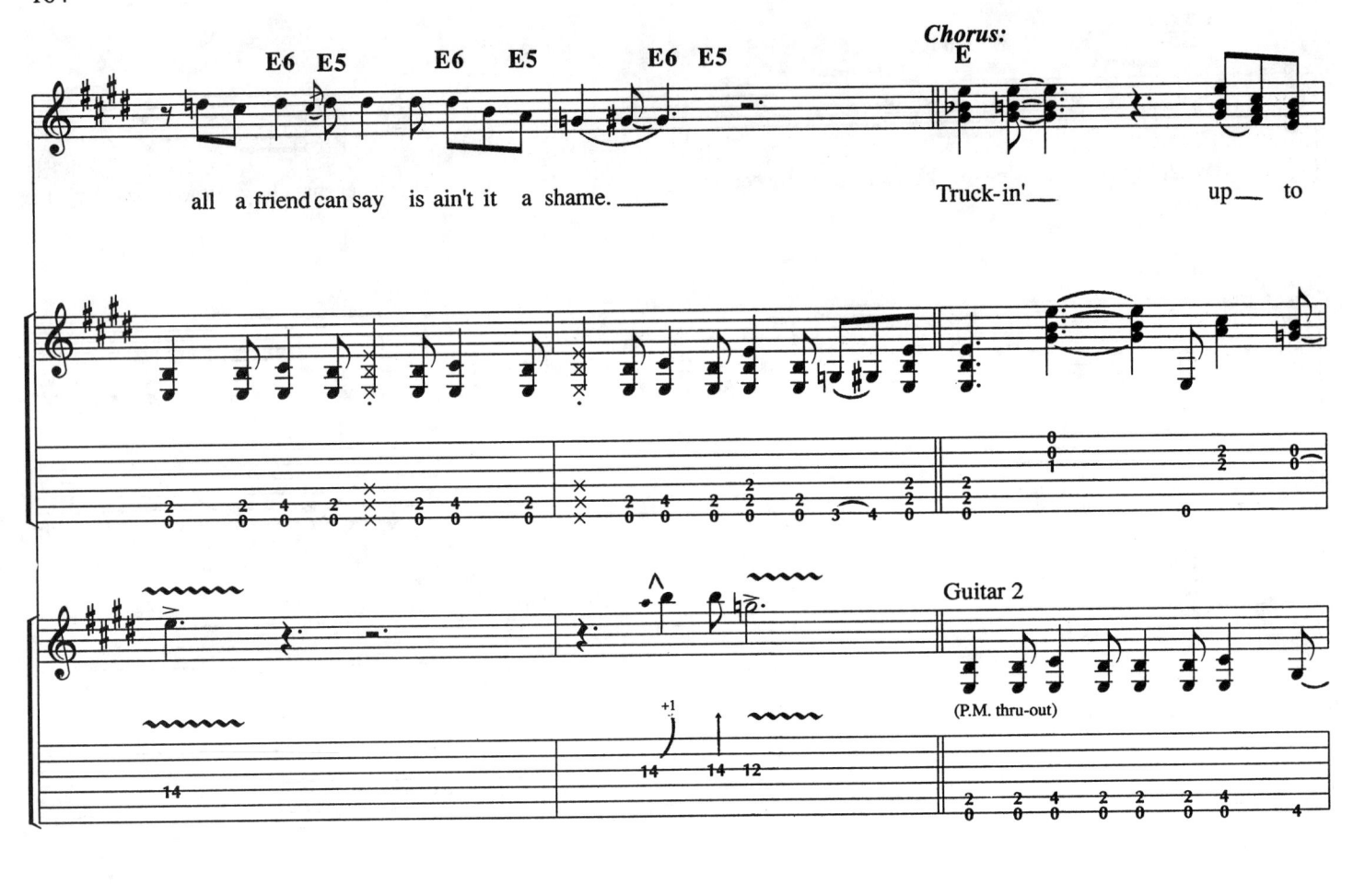

Takes time to pick a place to go, and just keep truck-in' on

Verse 4:

Sit-tin' an' star-in' out of the ho-tel win-dow, got a tip they're gon-na kick the door in a - gain I'd like to get some sleep be-fore I trav-el, but if you've got a war-rant, I guess you're gon-na come in.

Chorus:

Bust-ed down on Bour-bon street,

Guitar 3

set up___ like a bowl-in' pin,___ knocked down it gets to wear-ing___ thin,___ they just won't let___ you be.___

You're sick of hang-in' a-round 'an you'd like to trav-el, get tired of trav-el-in', you want to set-tle down I guess they can't re - voke your soul for try - in' Get

out of the door, light out and look all a - round.

171

172

Back home sit down and patch my bones and get back truck-in on

173

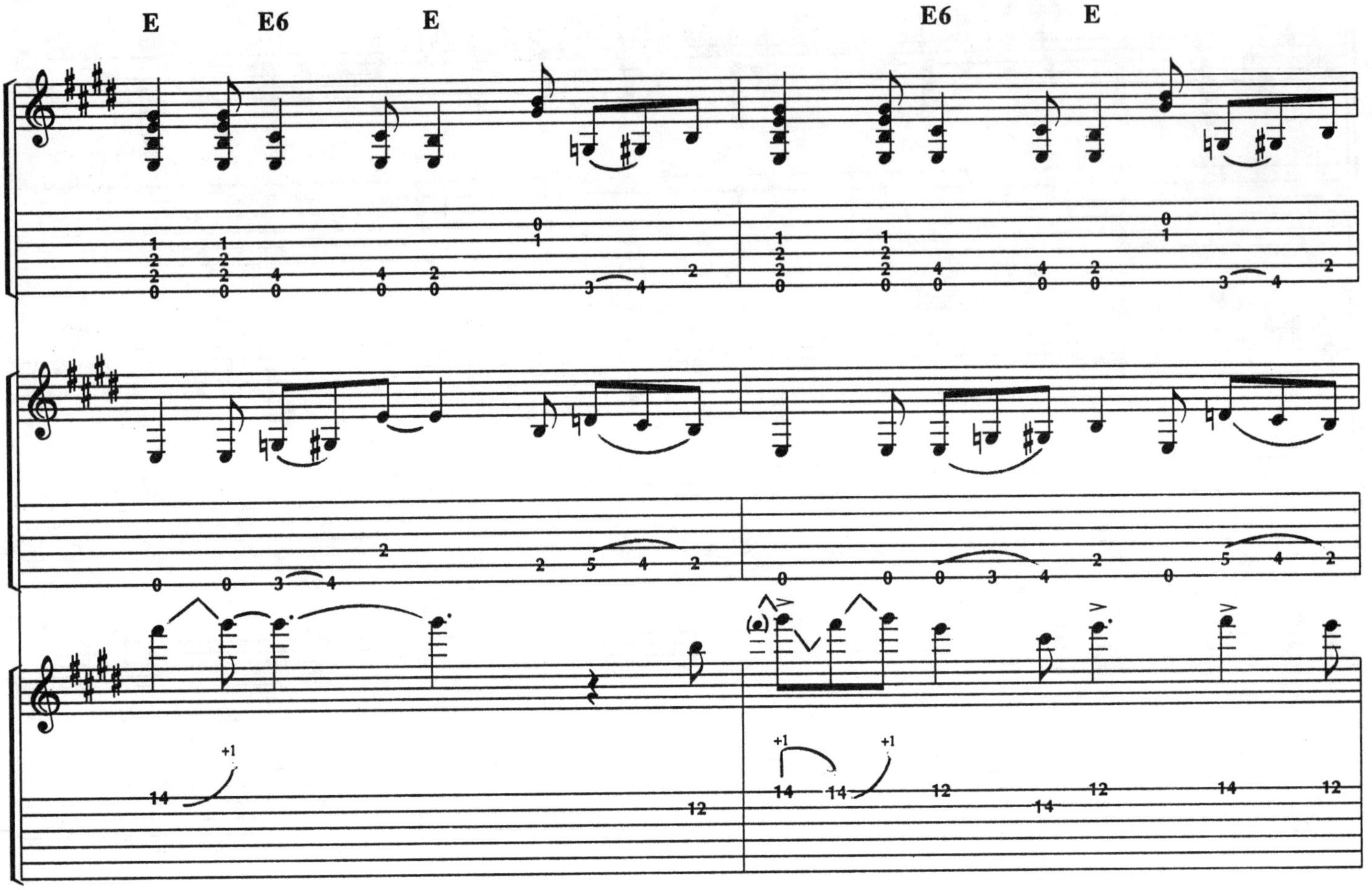
E
E6
E
E6
E

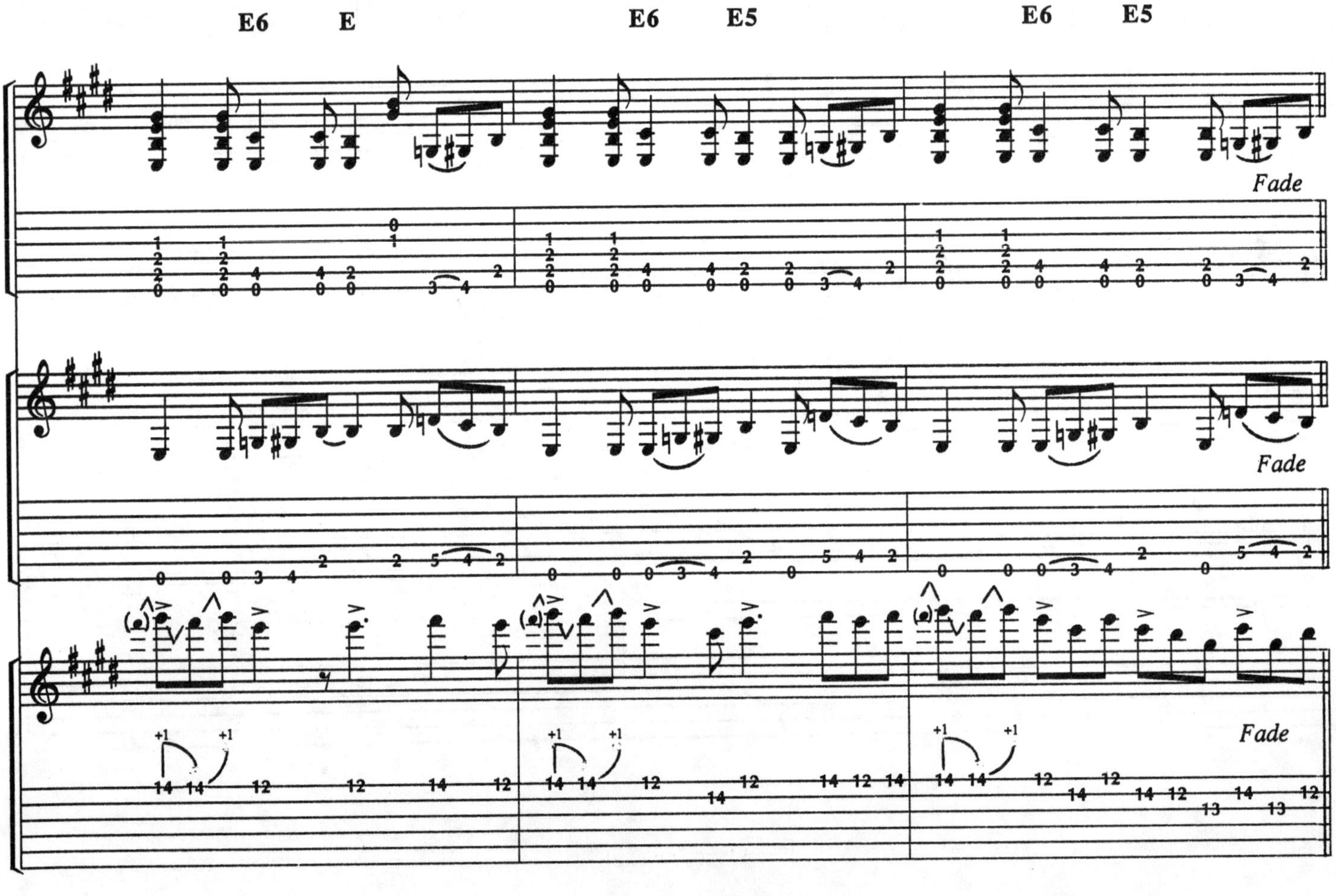
E6
E
E6
E5
E6
E5
Fade
Fade
Fade

UNCLE JOHN'S BAND

Words by
ROBERT HUNTER

Music by
JERRY GARCIA

176

Vocal

| G | D6 | C | D | **Verse 1:** | G |

Well, the first days__ are the hard-est days,__ don't you wor-ry an-y more. 'Cause__

| C | G |

Acoustic Guitar 1

Acoustic Guitar 2

Acoustic Guitar 3

Let ring

p

when life looks like eas-y street, there is dan-ger at your door

Think this through with me;

let me know your mind. Wo-oh, what I want to know is, are you kind?

179

Verse 2:

It's a buck danc-er's choice my friends; bet-ter take my ad-vice.

You know all the rules by now and the fire from the ice.

Will you come with me?

Won't you come with me? Wo - oh, what I want to know will you come with me?

God damn, well I de- clare, have you seen the like? Their

walls are made of can - non - balls;__ their__ mot - to is:__ "Don't tread___ on __ me."__

Chorus:

Come hear Un - cle John's band __

playing to the tide. Come with me or go alone, he's come to take his children home.

185

the same sto-ry the crow told me, it's the on-ly one he knows.

Like the morn-ing sun you come and

187

like the wind you go. Ain't no time to hate; bare-ly time to wait.

C D G D C D G
wo___ oh, ___ what I ___ want ___ to know: ___ where ___ does ___ the
p

Verse 4:
G
time ___ go?
I live ___ in a ___
P.M.

silver mine_ and I_ call it Beg - gar's Tomb.

I_ got_ me a vi - o - lin_ and I_ beg you call_ the tune.

Am
G
Em
An - y - bod - y's choice, —
V
VII
+1
+1
C
D
C
D
I can hear — your voice. —
No — oh, — what I —
Am7/C
V

want — to know — how — does — the song — go?

Chorus:
Come — hear Un-

cle John's Band — by the riv - er - side.

Got some things to talk — a - bout — here — be - side the ris -

ing___ tide.___ Come hear___ Un - cle John's Band___

play - ing to the tide.___ Come on a - long or go___

a - lone, he's come to take his chil - dren home.

Play 7 times

(Simile Guitar 2 on repeats)

Let ring

Let ring

*Bracketed, note 1st time only
**Guitar 2 plays Cm on 5th and 6th repeat

195

playing to the tide. Come on along or go alone, he's come to take his children home.

Dm
G
C
Dm
Da, da, da, da, da, da.
G
C
Dm
Da, da, da, da,— da, da.
(do, do, do, do.)
G
Dsus2/G
Da, da, da, da,— da, da.

GUITAR TAB GLOSSARY **

TABLATURE EXPLANATION

READING TABLATURE: Tablature illustrates the six strings of the guitar. Notes and chords are indicated by the placement of fret numbers on a given string(s).

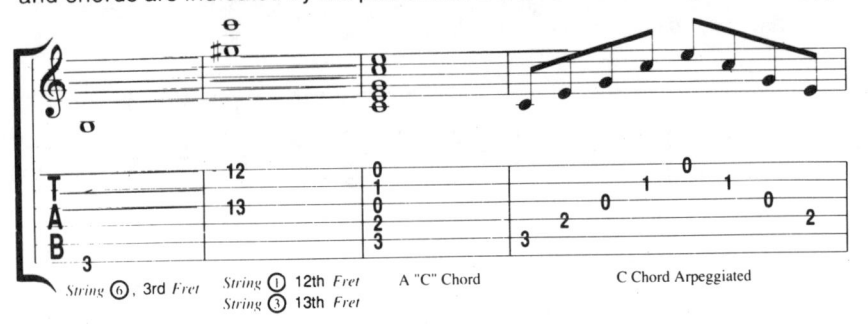

String ⑥, 3rd Fret
String ① 12th Fret
String ③ 13th Fret
A "C" Chord
C Chord Arpeggiated

BENDING NOTES

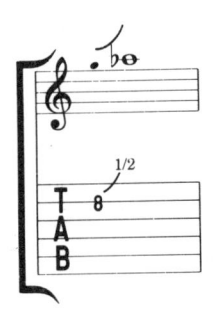

HALF STEP: Play the note and bend string one half step.*

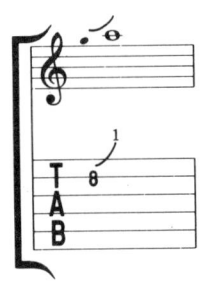

WHOLE STEP: Play the note and bend string one whole step.

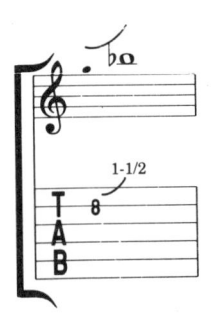

WHOLE STEP AND A HALF: Play the note and bend string a whole step and a half.

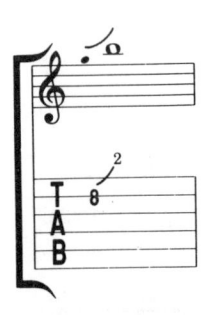

TWO STEPS: Play the note and bend string two whole steps.

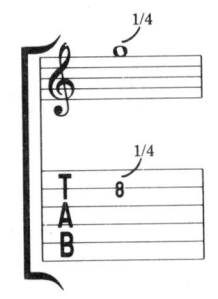

SLIGHT BEND (Microtone): Play the note and bend string slightly to the equivalent of half a fret.

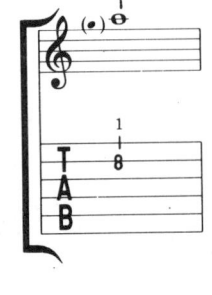

PREBEND (Ghost Bend): Bend to the specified note, before the string is picked.

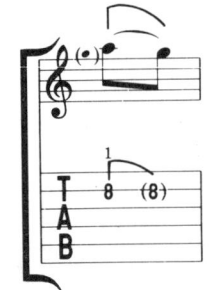

PREBEND AND RELEASE: Bend the string, play it, then release to the original note.

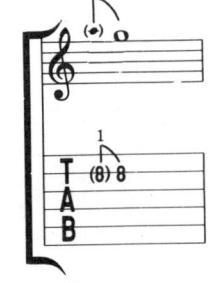

REVERSE BEND: Play the already-bent string, then immediately drop it down to the fretted note.

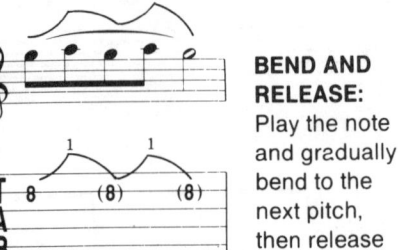

BEND AND RELEASE: Play the note and gradually bend to the next pitch, then release to the original note. Only the first note is attacked.

BENDS INVOLVING MORE THAN ONE STRING: Play the note and bend string while playing an additional note (or notes) on another string(s). Upon release, relieve pressure from additional note(s), causing original note to sound alone.

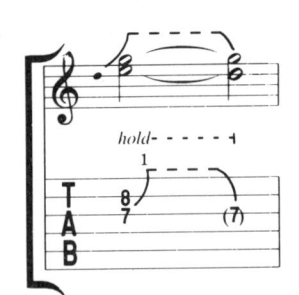

BENDS INVOLVING STATIONARY NOTES: Play notes and bend lower pitch, then hold until release begins (indicated at the point where line becomes solid).

UNISON BEND: Play both notes and immediately bend the lower note to the same pitch as the higher note.

DOUBLE NOTE BEND: Play both notes and immediately bend both strings simultaneously.

*A half step is the smallest interval in Western music; it is equal to one fret. A whole step equals two frets.

© 1990 Beam Me Up Music
c/o CPP/Belwin, Inc. Miami, Florida 33014
International Copyright Secured   Made in U.S.A.   All Rights Reserved

**By Kenn Chipkin and Aaron Stang

RHYTHM SLASHES

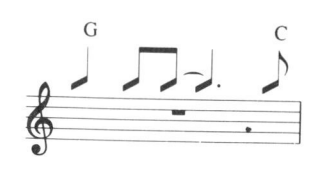

STRUM INDICATIONS: Strum with indicated rhythm. The chord voicings are found on the first page of the transcription underneath the song title.

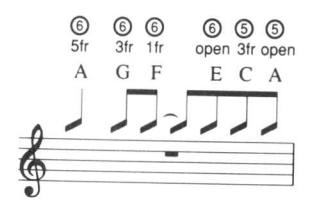

INDICATING SINGLE NOTES USING RHYTHM SLASHES: Very often single notes are incorporated into a rhythm part. The note name is indicated above the rhythm slash with a fret number and a string indication.

ARTICULATIONS

HAMMER ON: Play lower note, then "hammer on" to higher note with another finger. Only the first note is attacked.

LEFT HAND HAMMER: Hammer on the first note played on each string with the left hand.

PULL OFF: Play higher note, then "pull off" to lower note with another finger. Only the first note is attacked.

FRETBOARD TAPPING: "Tap" onto the note indicated by + with a finger of the pick hand, then pull off to the following note held by the fret hand.

TAP SLIDE: Same as fretboard tapping, but the tapped note is slid randomly up the fretboard, then pulled off to the following note.

BEND AND TAP TECHNIQUE: Play note and bend to specified interval. While holding bend, tap onto note indicated.

LEGATO SLIDE: Play note and slide to the following note. (Only first note is attacked).

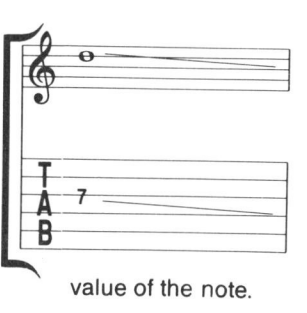

LONG GLISSANDO: Play note and slide in specified direction for the full value of the note.

SHORT GLISSANDO: Play note for its full value and slide in specified direction at the last possible moment.

PICK SLIDE: Slide the edge of the pick in specified direction across the length of the string(s).

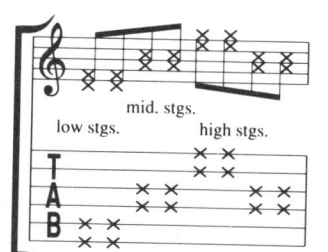

MUTED STRINGS: A percussive sound is made by laying the fret hand across all six strings while pick hand strikes specified area (low, mid, high strings).

PALM MUTE: The note or notes are muted by the palm of the pick hand by lightly touching the string(s) near the bridge.

TREMOLO PICKING: The note or notes are picked as fast as possible.

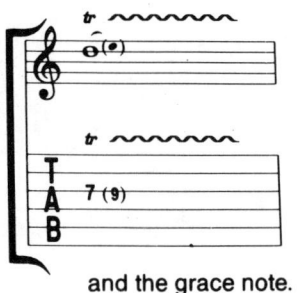

TRILL: Hammer on and pull off consecutively and as fast as possible between the original note and the grace note.

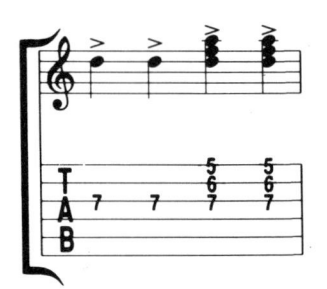

ACCENT: Notes or chords are to be played with added emphasis.

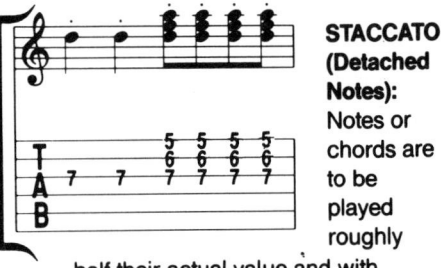

STACCATO (Detached Notes): Notes or chords are to be played roughly half their actual value and with separation.

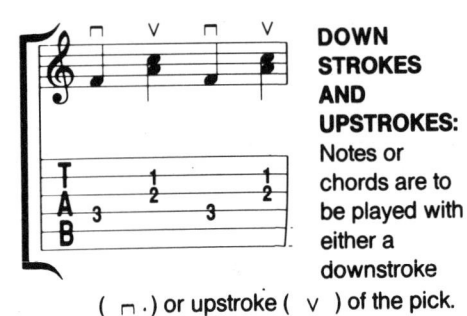

DOWN STROKES AND UPSTROKES: Notes or chords are to be played with either a downstroke (⊓) or upstroke (∨) of the pick.

VIBRATO: The pitch of a note is varied by a rapid shaking of the fret hand finger, wrist, and forearm.

HARMONICS

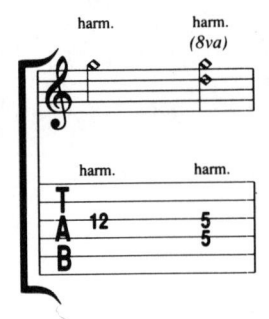

NATURAL HARMONIC: A finger of the fret hand lightly touches the note or notes indicated in the tab and is played by the pick hand.

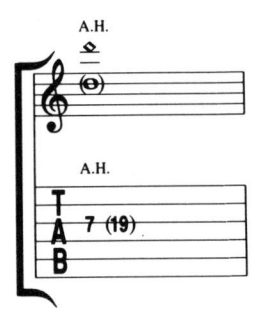

ARTIFICIAL HARMONIC: The first tab number is fretted, then the pick hand produces the harmonic by using a finger to lightly touch the same string at the second tab number (in parenthesis) and is then picked by another finger.

ARTIFICIAL "PINCH" HARMONIC: A note is fretted as indicated by the tab, then the pick hand produces the harmonic by squeezing the pick firmly while using the tip of the index finger in the pick attack. If parenthesis are found around the fretted note, it does not sound. No parenthesis means both the fretted note and A.H. are heard simultaneously.

TREMOLO BAR

SPECIFIED INTERVAL: The pitch of a note or chord is lowered to a specified interval and then may or may not return to the original pitch. The activity of the tremolo bar is graphically represented by peaks and valleys.

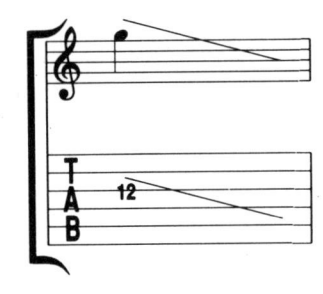

UN-SPECIFIED INTERVAL: The pitch of a note or a chord is lowered to an unspecified interval.